MW00745041

# THE PAIN
## —— OF A ——
# LITTLE GIRL

ANN MARIE A WILLIAMS

Copyright © 2021 by Ann Marie A Williams

Hardcover: 978-1-63767-431-4
Paperback: 978-1-63767-128-3
eBook: 978-1-63767-129-0
Library of Congress Control Number: 2021904471

All rights reserved. No part of this publication may be reproduced, distributed, or transmitted in any form or by any electronic or mechanical means, without the prior written permission of the publisher, except in the case of brief quotations embodied in critical reviews and certain other noncommercial uses permitted by copyright law.

This is a work of nonfiction.

Ordering Information:

 BookTrail Agency
8838 Sleepy Hollow Rd.
Kansas City, MO 64114

Printed in the United States of America

# Table of Contents

# Episode One

&

There was this family of five, a mother named Isabel, her three sons; Rick, Nick and Dex. And lastly her only daughter Felicia. Isabel was a single mother who was struggling to survive as a farmer to make ends meet. She took Felicia, her only daughter, when she was just four years old. And sent her off to live with her Grandmother who she accords as her mother. A woman whom she has never lived or grew up with and barely knew. Felicia was not pleased to go live with her Grandmother. But she had no choice but to start a new life with her grandmother called Mell, her husband, son Nathan and her two daughters, Keisha and Amanda. Felicia continued her life with a family she didn't know. She was not happy, and misses her mother and brothers. Felicia had always wanted to ask her mother why she sent her to live with Grandma Mell.

Some years passed and Felicia turned seven years old, and one day she decided to visit her mother after school. Isabel was surprised to see her, and asked her why she was here. Felicia said, *"Why did you take me to live with Grandma Mell and her family, when you barely know her?!"* Isabel replied, *"Because the school is closer to her house. That's the reason!"* Then Felicia told her mother that she was not happy living there. but Isabel told Felicia to go back to her grandmother. Felicia begged and cried to her mother not to take her to grandmother but that proved futile.

Felicia left and went back to Grandma Mell's house. It was late when Felicia got home and Grandma Mell asked why she came home that late. Felicia replied that she went to see her mother at her house. Grandma Mell went into her room, got a belt and beat Felicia for visiting her mother. She then told her not to go there again. Despite the beating, Felicia was determined not to give up until Isabel took her back home.

Felicia continues this almost every evening. Sometimes instead of Isabel telling her to leave, and will get her older brother Rick to run her down to go back. Felicia will often cry and wonder if your Mother ever wanted or loved her. She didn't like living with Grandma Mell. But Felicia will not go back to Grandma Mell house at times. So sometimes would visit her schoolmates. and lie to sleep at their houses. She would even wait until people fell asleep at night and sleep on their porch or sometimes under their houses in her school uniform. She was so afraid and frightened. When Felicia goes back to Grandma Mell's house, she would be beaten by Grandma Mell. but Felicia doesn't care what happens to her. All she wanted was for mother to take her back and take care of her. But all Isabel's time was for her last two sons Dex and Nick and their father who was already married to another woman.

Another year went by living with Grandma Mell and Felicia turned 8 years old. She started washing her own clothes, carrying water, cleaning the house and yard. Grandma was always working and would leave the house as early as 6: 00

am and would not return until night, around 7: 00 to 7: 30 pm. When she gets home, She will send Keisha and Amanda along with Felicia to go buy oil or coals for her to cook something for them to eat. Sometimes when the three go to the shop. Keisha and Amanda would meet up with their boyfriends and have Felicia wait for them by the roadside. she would sit there waiting for them until they finished with what they were doing. Felicia was afraid to tell Grandma Mell what was happening because the girls threatened her.

One day Amanda and Keisha came up with a plan to break in around the neighborhood. They planned to break into this particular house and steal. They told Felicia that she has to go with them. Felicia didn't want to take any part in their plan, but Keisha threatened her to make up lies about her to tell Grandma Mell. Felicia was afraid that Grandma Mell would beat her if Keisha told her lies, so she had no other choice then to follow them. Later that day the three of them came home for lunch, they went into a lady's house and stole some snacks. After that every day they started doing it for weeks. Eventually, they got caught. The three of them got in trouble with Grandma Mell. The lady demanded that Grandma Mell pay her back for everything that they had stolen or else she was going to involve the police. Grandma Mell begged her not to involve the police. After that Grandma Mell was really upset with the girls and beat them with a leather belt. But, even after that Keisha, Amanda and Felicia continue to steal from the neighborhood. One dayThey even woke up Felicia at 4; 00 am in the morning to go under the neighbors' mango trees and their cocoa trees. They continued this for a while. Until one of the neighbors suspected someone coming early in the morning to pick up mangoes from his tree.

So, one morning he decided to wait and hide to find out who was taking his mangoes. Amanda and Felicia didn't realize the man was there waiting for them. So they started to pick up the mangoes, when the man came out of his hiding. They ran but the man chased after them. When Felicia ran, she fell and hurt her leg. She started to cry but Amanda continued running, when they reached home Amanda started to blame felicia and told her it is her fault she got hurt.

Grandma Mell's son, Nathan lived two houses apart from their house with his cousin Blue and his Grandma Jones. Blue was not around often. He was working on a boat and was making a lot of money. The three girls always go to their house to take food for Grandma Jones. Amanda knows where Blue kept his money and tells Keisha, so they plan on how they are going to break into the house and steal the money. Felicia overheard them speaking and told them she was going to tell Grandma Mell, Keisha threatened Felicia again that if she told Grandma Mell or their dad, she would push Felicia over the wall into the river by their house, and make it look like an accident. Felicia was so afraid of her, so decided not to say anything to their dad or Grandma Mell. Amanda and Keisha already had their plan all sorted out. One Thursday morning after Grandma Mell left for work, Keisha woke Amanda up and Felicia and told them what her plan was when they came home for lunch. They did their morning chores and got themselves ready and off to school. But Felicia was not happy with their plan.

At school she was very nervous and couldn't concentrate on her work at school. She was even thinking not to go home for lunch. But she remembered she was threatened by Keisha. Felicia went home for lunch; the girls were home for lunch as well. Keisha asked if they were ready and Amanda said yes, but Felicia didn't answer. After finishing their lunch, the three girls went over to Nathan's Grandma house. Keisha picked the lock and opened up the room and sent Felicia in the house and Keisha told where the money was in a suitcase under his bed. Amanda was by the gate looking to see if anyone was coming while Keisha and Felicia in the house getting the money. There was a lot of money in the suitcase rolled up like one hundred dollars bills. Keisha told Felicia to take out five hundred dollars and she did and put back the rest in a suitcase and they put back everything in a hurry and locked back the door. And they left in a hurry, after they were safe, they shared the money among themselves. They gave Felicia a $100 bill, Amanda and Keisha got $200 each. Felicia went back to school and showed her friends the money she had just stolen so they went to a nearby shop to buy things with her friends.

The shopkeeper noticed that Felicia had a $100 bill in her hands, so when the shopkeeper asked where she got it from, Felicia said that her auntie gave her the money. The shopkeeper asked why her auntie would give a seven-year-old a $100 bill and the shopkeeper took the money and told Felicia if she wants her money back, she has to bring her mom and she told Felicia and her friends to go back to school. Felicia was mad that evening when she was coming home Amanda and Keisha asked what she had bought with the money. Felicia shouted: "Nothing!!!, *because the shopkeeper took the money and told me to bring my mom if I want it back!*" Amanda and Keisha started laughing at Felicia and tells her that she is very stupid. Felicia started crying and told them to leave her alone.

Two weeks later, Amanda and Keisha went back to Nathan Grandma's house to steal more money but they didn't take Felicia with them this time. So that evening when grandma Mell came home. One of Amanda's friends' mom came to the house and told grandma Mell her daughter came home with money and other stuff. And she asked her where she got them from, she said Amanda had money at school sharing with her friends.

Grandma Mell was so surprised to learn where Amanda got the money from. So that night she called Amanda and asked her where she got the money she had at school, sharing it with her friends. And she said Keisha gives her the money. Grandma Mell called Keisha and asked her where she got the money from and she said that she found it. Grandma Mell asked her why you didn't tell me and where you found it and when, she said two weeks ago down the road, and she was afraid to tell her. But grandma Mell knew she was lying so she called Felicia and asked her if she knew anything about the money Keisha found. But Felicia was so afraid to talk to grandma Mell. She started to cry and said it was not me that took the money.

Grandma Mell tells them if they don't tell the truth she is going to beat them. Amanda told her they broke into Grandma Jones house and stole Blue money in his suitcase.

*What!!!* shout Grandma Mell, *how much money did you guys take? she asked them.* And Felicia said the first time they made me take five hundred dollars. *They gave me one hundred dollars and Mrs. Mack from the shop to my school took it from me, and said I must bring my mom to collect it from her.* Grandma Mell was very angry with the girls and started to beat them with a leat belt. She told them if they will do something like this again and if they don't stop, that she will kill them.

She tells them that she is going to make Nathan beat them again, when he comes over to the house in the morning. Grandma Mell refuses to give them any food so they go to bed hungry that night. Amanda and Keisha were so angry at Felicia, they told her we hated you so much, so Felicia again cried and said she wanted to go back to her mother. Grandma Mell heard her and shouted at her and said shut up and go to bed. The next morning when Nathan came to the house Grandma Mell told what happened. He called the girls and asked them why they went and took Blue money. So, he got a piece of wire and beat the three girls. Felicia's belly got cut by the wire he beat her with.

Grandma Mell told them; *I hope this beating will teach you not to break into people's houses.* Felicia still wonders why her mom Isabel chose to live with these monsters. She feels like taking her own life. Because she was not happy at all, but had no choice but to stay despite everything. She will still run away after school and go to her mom Isabel house but she will beat her and send her son Rick to run her back.

Keisha went to secondary school while Amanda and Felicia were still going to primary school. But Kesha's first 2 years in secondary school she was about 14 years old and got pregnant. Grandma Mell finds out and asks her who is responsible for the pregnancy and she tells her a guy named Luther and Grandma Mell beat her with the pregnancy. One day, Kesha brings Luther to the house and introduces him to everyone at home, and Grandma Mell loves him and welcomes him. Before you know it, he starts to sleep over at night in the same room she shares with Amanda and Felicia. Sometimes they will have intercourse while Amanda and Felicia are there, at times not sleeping yet.

One day Grandma Mell called Felicia and she answered, *Yes!!!* and she asked who she was answering yes to when she called her and slapped her in the face and said ``don't answer me yes when I call you." Felicia got mad and hated grandma Mell for that. Grandma Mell will always treat her badly and will beat her for every little thing. Felicia said to herself one day why this woman always likes to beat her so much.

She asked God why my mother sent me to die at a young age from the hands of a woman and her children. She didn't even live with her or know her that much. Felicia said who will have her only daughter and give her away to a mad and crazy woman like this, who loves to beat and fight her own husband. Felicia will always cry and will tell the neighbor's daughters what is happening to her. And they will ask her why don't you go and live with her mother. But she told them that she doesn't think her mom Isabel loves and wants her. That's why she sent her here to live with. Grandma Mell will fight her husband all the time when he comes home drunk. Sometimes she will cut him and trap him so that he will have to go to the hospital.

A few days later, Felicia decided to run away and go to look for Isabel's dad. Felicia was getting ready for school. She packed her book bag with some of her clothing, she was just 9 and a half years old at the time. She walked that morning to the city and went to the bus terminal. Felicia asked a conductor where she could get a bus going to the village of mount view. He said to her right over there, that red one will take you there.

She gets on the bus, the bus leaves the terminal, it will take a while to reach where Felicia was going. Felicia didn't really have a clue where she was supposed to get off. She came off the second to last stop in number nine. It was about 6pm in the evening. So Felicia saw one lady and she asked if she knew where her grandfather Raphael lived. But the lady told her she didn't know him, and where Raphael lived, Felicia said mount view, so the lady told her you pass it already is the other village before number nine.

The lady asked her how old she was. She said, 'I am 10 years old'. The lady asked her where is your mother she said at home. Did she know that you are here looking for your grandfather? Felicia replied yes. She sent me to look for him. The lady realizes nothing is adding up so she takes her to a nearby police station. And told the policemen that this little girl seems like she has run away, looking for her grandfather Raphael in mount view. The police officer asked her what her name was, and she said Felicia. He also asked about the name of his mother, and she answered that her mother is called Isabel. The police officer called the central police station in the town and reported that Felicia ran away with a book bag with some clothing in it. That was around 8pm in the night. Mom Isabel and Grandma Mell went to the Central police station making a report that her daughter Felicia is missing and they can't find her. The police told them they just got a call that she is at Mount View police station and they are going to bring her up tonight in the police transportation. Felicia arrived at the Central police station.

When Mom Isabel and Grandma Mell were waiting for her. Mom Isabel asked her where she said looking for your dad, but Grandma Mell pulled her by her ear and said you need some good beating. Felicia was so afraid to go home with Grandma Mell. She asked mom Isabel if she could spend the night with her and she said yes. Felicia was a bit happy and felt relieved. Grandma Mell told mom Isabel ``see you tomorrow when I come to get Felicia" then they went home, Felicia had a shower and something to eat and went to bed. The next day when Felicia woke up, she was happy to see her brothers and had breakfast with them. Isabel asked her why she ran away from her grandma and she said that they kept beating her and treating bad. She shows her the bruises on her skin but mom Isabel didn't believe her. So that morning around 10 am. Grandma Mell came to the house and she and Isabel were talking. What Felicia didn't know was that they already had a plan for her. They called Felicia in the yard, and Grandma Mel had a Greta in her hand. There were two good sized stones in the yard. Grandma Mell put the Greta next to the two stones, told Felicia to kneel down on the Greta, and gave her the 2 stones in her hands and told her to lift them up in the air. Felicia started to cry and asked her mother why she is doing this to her. Isabel said for you to stop running away and for you to behave yourself and listen to her grandma Mell. Felicia was there under the hot sun for about two hours. Her knees were hurting so bad and her hands. Felicia hated her Grandma and mother. She said to herself that will not stop her. That evening Felicia went back home with grandma Mell.

Felicia was about nine years old, she decided she was not giving up until she got her mother to take her back to live with her this time. So, one morning Felicia left her Grandma Mell house with the intention of going to see her mom Isabel. After school, again to convince her to take her back. Unfortunately, that evening, things didn't work out the way Felicia expected it would be for her. When Mom Isabel saw her, she asked Felicia, What Are you doing up here this evening?" Felicia said to her, *'I want to come back home to stay with you and my brothers'*. But mom Isabel chases her with a stick and sends her back to grandma Mell house. But Felicia refused and ran out the yard. This time she really decided she was not going back to Grandma Mell's house.

So that evening she chilled out on the street, where her mother couldn't find her until night. Felicia's father's mom was living right around the corner away from her mother's house. Felicia went to mother may, her father's mother's house around 8pm. She knocked on the door and her grandma came out and asked who was there. And Felicia replied, *"it's me, mother may."* and she asked what she was doing here this time of night in your school uniform. Felicia told her what happened, so Mother May not be happy at all, but she takes Felicia and gives her something to eat and get her cleaned up, so she stays there for the night. The next morning when Felicia woke up Mother May told her to go back to her Mom Isabel to get ready for school. But instead Felicia decided to take a shortcut to another road. On her way there she saw some people she knew and followed them up the mountain. But they never knew she was following them. But they never knew she was following them. After about 20 minutes one of the ladies noticed her next to their hut. The lady asked her," what was she doing here?" Felicia told her," I followed you all up here." And she explained to them what happened to her. They allowed her to spend the day at the mountain with them. But mom Isabel's friend's granddaughter was therewith them. Felicia knew her. It was getting dark and time for them to go back home. Felicia went home with mom Isabel's friend's granddaughter that evening. The girl's grandmother was happy to see Felicia and hugged and said, *"Today is your day"*. But Felicia was like what's going on. The girl's grandmother said, "Your mother went to grandma Mell house to get stuff and you're not going to live with grandma Mell ever again. Felicia was so happy and glad. She was jumping for joy and crying. The girl's grandmother said," go up and meet your mom, she is waiting for you. But Felicia was afraid mom Isabel would beat her, but when her mother saw her, she was happy and hugged her and welcomed her back home.

# Episode Two

※

nother life began for Felicia with her mother Isabel, her two brothers and the mother's boyfriend, Tim. He works as a baker in a bakery down the street like four blocks away from the house. He loves to smoke a lot of cigarettes. And he had another woman and children. When he was not working, he spent lots of time at the house. Felicia was about ten years old at the time. And she didn't like Tim that much. Felicia was looking big and mature for her age at ten. Tim will sometimes bump into Felicia, and his hand will touch her breast, and he will apologize. But Felicia was feeling uncomfortable about it. One other day she went outside in the bath to take a shower, when she saw Tim at the window peeking at her.

That evening when Isabel got home from the farm, Felicia wanted to talk to her about it. Isabel agreed to talk to her. Felicia said, *'It's about Tim, he always bumped into me sometimes and when I am bathing, he is pecking at me from the window. I don't like it, and I am not feeling comfortable with it'*. But later that night, Isabel had a talk with Tim about what Felicia told her. But he denied every bit of it, and Isabel believed him over Felicia. Felicia's life was like hell with Tim after Isabel told him what she said.

As time went by, Tim was not a very nice person to Felicia and her big brother Rick. Especially when Isabel was not around. He cooked the food, and told them before they could eat the food that he would rather put chicken poo in the food and give them to eat. But they will not eat from the food he cooks. Felicia told her mom Isabel about it, but she never believed her. Mom Isabel is always busy at the farm mountain most of the time. She never spent much time with Felicia and her brothers.

Felicia didn't really know her dad. But one day she asked her mother about her dad and why they were not together. Isabel said to Felicia that there's nothing to tell about her dad. Also, she said he is worthless and a lying bastard. Felicia asked where he is now and where he is living. Isabel told her that he is living somewhere on the other side of the Island called Mayra. Felicia asks her mother whether she can go and visit her dad. Isabel agreed to Felicia's request but she can go with her Grandmother May.

Later that evening she went to see her dad's mother, Grandma May and told her she wanted to go and visit her dad. Grandma May said she was going there in two days and she could go with her. *I will inform your dad that you are coming with me, said grandma May.* Felicia was so excited to go and meet her dad for the first time at age ten. Felicia is back to her mother's house and tells them with excitement that Grandma May is going in two days and she will go with her. That night Felicia packed some clothing in her bag and went to bed.

The second morning, she wakes up very early, dresses and eats breakfast. Then it was time for her to leave, she hugged and kissed her mother, and her two brothers, Rick and Nick. She walked down the street to meet Grandma May. The taxi came and took them to the boat deck. They were on the boat at 10:45 am but the boat left at 11 am. Felicia was a bit scared because she never rode in a boat before. Even that day on the boat Grandma May introduced her to one guy on the boat as her brother named Maf, one of her father's older sons.

It takes six hours to get to the island where her dad lives. They finally reached the place where they had to take a small fishing boat over to the island. They get a ride up to the village, where Felicia's dad was working. He was working at his brother's restaurant and bar. When Felicia and Grandma May got there, she was so nervous about meeting her dad. A big black man came out and hugged her and Grandma May. After they sat down around the table, he asked her how she was doing and she responded that she was fine.

Grandma May introduced Felicia to the big course man as her father. Her dad said to her that she has grown big and beautiful. He got them something to eat. Two more men came over where she and Grandma May were sitting and hugged Grandma may. She said to Felicia that they were two of her other sons, therefore your uncles, Lewis and John. Felicia greeted them. They asked how her mother was doing and she said she was fine. Then her dad came with the food for both of them and they ate. Felicia's dad went and got some drinks and two beers for his two brothers also.

Later that evening, they all left to go to their house. Grandma May went to stay with her sister and Felicia went to her father's house. She was not happy about going to stay with her father because she did not know him but when they got there, she felt at home. There was no light in the house, they were using a small oil lamp. When they got in the yard there was this woman, and 6 children, 3 boys and 3 girls. Felicia said hello to them and they responded. Felicia's dad said to her they are your brothers and sisters. Looking at the vast family she felt that was the reason her father abandoned her. Felicia has spent two weeks with her father and her siblings, she got to know and enjoy her stay with them. It was time for her to go back home. Her dad gave her 50 dollars and some cod fish to go back home with.

In the morning, It was time to leave and Felicia hugs her siblings and their mom and tells them goodbye. She and her dad left to meet up with Grandma May at the deck. She hugged her dad and said bye to him as well and he told her to take care of herself.

Grandma May and Felicia and others went across in a small boat to take the big boat back to the mainland. They finally reached their destination. Isabel asked Felicia how she spent her time with her dad and his family, and she said not too bad. He gave me this money and some fish, she said. Felicia gave the money to her mother and asked the mother whether she can go again during vacation.

Felicia continued her life. She went to school. Tim the baker was home alone, her brothers were over the road playing marbles with their friends. While Isabel was still at the farm, Felicia came back from school and went in the bedroom to change her school uniform, when Tim entered the bedroom and started to touch her. She tried to pull away from him. but he grabbed her and said I was watching you for a long time and I meant to do this to you, and he ripped her clothes off and defiled her. She cried a lot and screamed aloud, but Tim covered her mouth totally, so no one heard her scream. There was blood on Felicia's body. He told her to go in the bath and shower, and if she tells anyone, she and her brothers will die. Tim cleaned up the ground where he defiled her.

Felicia was in the bath still crying and asked God why this was happening to her and wanted to kill herself. Because if she tried to tell her mother, she wouldn't believe her. This kept happening for about two months just to get food for herself and her brothers. Felicia was tired of Tim and his threats and decided to tell her mother finally. She went to Isabel one evening; Tim was at work. She was crying and asked Isabel why she can have a man in the house who defiles her daughter constantly. Isabel was shocked to hear this and couldn't believe that Tim would do this to her only daughter.

The next morning when he came to the house, Isabel confronted him about it, and he denied it again. And she put his things outside, and told him never to come any way around her and her family. If he does so, she will call the police to arrest him. He takes his stuff and leaves. Two days later, Isabel apologized to Felicia for not listening and believing her. And she told her, she will never let this happen to her again. Mom Isabel gives her a hug and tells her sorry. Then everything was fine with the family, but not for Felicia. She was in so much pain and traumatized by what had happened to her.

The School was about to go on holiday break, and Felicia wanted to go and revisit her dad and his family again. She asked Isabel if she could go. Isabel thought it was a good idea for her to go. She was a bit excited to go because she wanted to talk to her dad about what happened to her. She went to visit her dad all by herself this time. She finally got there, and her father was happy to see her and her siblings. She greeted them and was glad to see them again. Felicia and her dad were starting to get along well.

One day, Felicia's dad was home, so she went to him and asked him whether they could talk. He responded yes to her. She asked him why he abandoned her and her mother. He said he never abandoned her. Things didn't work out for her mother and him, and things were not working out for him on the mainland, so he had to move away. Felicia further asked him why he never looked for her and even checked up on her. *'Isabel gave me away at age four to a woman she hardly knows. My life was a living hell, and I have a father who never looked for me and cared about me to know if I was alive or dead,'* she said to her father. She told him what she went through as a little girl and was even molested by mom Isabel's ex-boyfriend. The dad shouted in anger and was hurt but asked for Felicia's forgiveness, and he hugged. He explained that he had another child with Isabel, a boy, but he died, and we had you, but he was not good enough for her mother. He was already married and had two daughters with his ex-wife and five more children with five different women. He said in the earlier days when he used to sail on bulk boats and make lots of money. But he did love Isabel very much. But she didn't want him because she thought he was a cheat and a liar.

Felicia still doesn't know what all this has to do with him abandoning her. She asked her dad, why don't you take me to live with you and your family. Isabel will never give you to me, even your Grandma May asked her for you and she refused. She was surprised. Felicia continues her visit with her dad and his family until one day something happens. One evening, Felicia's dad came home from work; he sat down by the table to eat his dinner and called Felicia to eat with him from his plate. He did it a few times, But the stepmom didn't like it. and said something about why he always takes that little brat at the table every time he is eating. What happens to her own children? The dad took the plate with the food and threw it at the stepmom, and he started to beat her up in front of the children and Felicia. The children will try to fight him off their mother. But Felicia was scared.

It was not the first time he hit her, she didn't seem like she liked Felicia and none of the dad's children, which were not hers. Every time he gives anything to his children outside the home, they will fight and argue over it. Felicia was just praying for her time to hurry up and go back home to Isabel. She wondered if her father ever loved her and if he ever noticed that she was hurting so much. He did not even spend much time with her. She wondered what it would be like for her. Her time was up to go back home, and her dad packed her with a bag of rice, some fish and 50 dollars. Not enough money to help with school. And sent her back to Isabel.

# Episode Three

༄

When Felicia came back from visiting her dad, she was about ten and a half years old at the time. Isabel now has a new boyfriend named Mr. Ash, who moves in to live with her and the children. Felicia asked her, *'you promised you will not bring another man to the house to live with us, after what Tim the baker did, and you didn't do anything'*. She said, *'he is a nice person and you guys will get along well with him'*. Felicia likes him and hopes he will not be like Tim. Mr. Ash had a good job to help clean up the city. Sometimes he will go to the farm mountain with Isabel to help her with the farming. He has a daughter down the street with a lady he was living with and works at the same place. The lady will always argue with him to take care of their daughter.

He smokes and drinks, and will always stop by a shop down the road. Sometimes, he will come home drunk. For the first one and a half years, Mr. Ash was doing great until he started drinking and coming home drunk. Felicia and her big brother sometimes have to help him when he throws up. When he gets home at times, Isabel refuses to help him and will say to him, 'look at you'. He will thank Felicia after helping him when he comes home drunk.

One day Felicia was home alone; Mr. Ash got home from work drunk and asked her where everyone was. Isabel went out, and the boys were over the road with their friends playing. He came and sat down on the chair next to Felicia and started touching her. He said to her, *I've been watching you, and you look like a mature woman*. She said to him, *I am only eleven and a half years old*. He said to her, *I will give money and buy nice stuff for you, and you must not tell anyone*. She said to him, *I don't want your money, just leave me alone, you drunk bastard, and get off of me*. But he keeps grabbing her close to him and tries to take her clothes off. But She insists on continuing to keep on struggling with him to let her go.

Felicia started to cry and told him to stop and let her go. Finally, her big brother Rick came into the house and saw him trying to force himself on his sister. Rick grabbed him and pushed him down the floor. Mr. Ash said to both of them, you people will suffer in this house. Rick told him, *any time you try something like this to my sister again. I will kill you myself, and you better believe I will*. He said to him again, *we will not tell mom Isabel what happens here today because she will not believe us over you. But if you ever try it again, she will bury you and believe us.*

Felicia went outside behind the house crying. She was thankful to God for sending her brother on time, while Mr. Ash and Rick were still in the house arguing. Later that evening mom Isabel gets home, nobody said anything to her. But someone told her that the children and Mr. Ash were arguing earlier in the house. Mr. Ash was fast asleep, and she woke him up and asked him what happened today. He said, ask your children, I don't remember anything that happened. Felicia wanted to tell her what happened, but Rick shook his head and said no.

Two months passed, but things were never the same again with Felicia, Rick and Mr. Ash. Rick gets into a fight with Mr. Ash, and all Isabel can say to them is she doesn't want any fight in her house. But things were never the same in the home again. Isabel was always spending most of her time farming and was not there to know what was going on with her children.

Felicia was not doing well in school, she was always fighting with her schoolmates and getting into trouble. The children in Felicia's class were divided into groups, fighting and cursing for weeks. one day, She had a ring that her dad gave to her, and she lent it to her best friend Jenna in the morning during the first period until lunchtime. After school call in for the afternoon period, Felicia asked back for the ring, but Jenna said it is lost and she cannot find it, so Felicia was mad at her and said to her best-friend, *'if you don't bring back my ring, I will beat you up after school is closed'.*

When school dismissed that evening, one schoolmate ambushed Jenna on Felicia, and she got into a fight with her. Felicia beat her, and her face was dinged up and was bleeding. After the fight, everyone went their way. But later that evening, when Jenna got home, her mom asked what happened to her face, and she said she and Felicia were fighting. Jenna's mom called mom Isabel and told her what happened between the two girls. Mom Isabel and Jenna's mom talk about the situation. Then they put the two of them on the phone so they can apologize to each other, and they told them they didn't want them to be fighting with each other because they are best of friends.

Still, at school, Felicia was giving trouble. One evening after school, she and the girl of the other group got into a fight in the school yard. One of the teachers broke up the fight between both girls and sent everyone to their home. So, the next morning Felicia was mad and decided to walk with a knife at school. She showed the knife to everyone in her group. After lunch that day, she and the same girl were going to fight again. When the girl brother was trying to break up the fight. She cut him on his hand with the knife she had taken to school. She got in trouble and was sent to the principal office. Later that day, the girls in the class were called to the office and were warned to stop fighting in school. Felicia and the other girl got suspended from school for two weeks with a letter from the Principal. And before they can return back to school, they have to bring their parents.

When Felicia went home, she told her mother what happened and gave her the letter from the principal. She said that she is not going anywhere with her. Felicia asked her why she doesn't want to do anything for her even though she is the only daughter and treats her as if she is nobody. *What have I done to you?* She asked, *where is the love you are supposed to have for me? All I see you care about is your younger son Nick. Not me, your only daughter, not Rick and you even gave Dex to his father. Sometimes I wish I was dead because not even my father cares about me too.*

At age 12, she was still home from school. She had her eyes on one of the neighbor's sons named Sam. He always liked her also, but he was older than her, but they would talk at times. But this day, Felicia was at home by herself; everyone else was away. Sam came to her house that day, and they talked, and he asked her, where's your mom and stepfather? She said, mom Isabel went to the farm, and Mr. Ash is at work. They were behind the house, and Sam came up to her and kissed her and touched her up and she said to him to stop and push him off, but he insisted that he loved her and he wanted to be with her alone. He started to kiss her again, and he held her by her hand and went into the house and had intercourse with her. After they finished, he kissed her and went to his house.

After that day, Felicia was so in love with him. They had intercourse twice again after. She was home for almost one month before Mr. Ash went with her back to school. After school, Felicia will go to her friend's house and get home late; Isabel wondered where Felicia goes after school. Three months later, Isabel noticed she was looking different and gaining weight and said something was wrong. Isabel asked her if she could be pregnant. The next morning Felicia was getting ready for school. When mom Isabel came to the bedroom and asked who was responsible for the pregnancy and who she was having intercourse with. Felicia told her what she was talking about. And she wants to go to school.

Felicia was feeling mad and upset with Isabel and blamed her for everything that happened to her. She told her she is never around for her and why she cares what happens to her now. Felicia didn't want to talk to mom Isabel about it, but mom Isabel didn't give up until she told her that it was Sam, the next-door neighbor's son. Mom Isabel sent and called Sam, so when he came, she asked him in-front of her, but she ran in the house and started to cry. And Sam left and said he would come back in the evening. Later that day, Sam came back, and Felicia was ready to talk. Isabel asked her who she was pregnant for, and she said Sam, but he said in front of her he never had intercourse with her and he left the yard without saying another word. And went his way. Isabel was so upset about the matter and decided she would talk to his mom Mrs. B the next day.

But when mom Isabel approached her, she said not her son. And mom Isabel must go and find the father for her daughter's pregnancy and tell her daughter to stop calling her son's name in her mix-up. But both parents were cursing in the road about their children. Isabel said she is under-age and she is going to the police. Mrs. B went her way, and mom Isabel took Felicia to the police station and complained her daughter is just 12 years old and is pregnant for one of her neighbor's sons called Sam, who is 19 years old.

But later that day, Sam was arrested by police and was taken to the police station for questioning about the matter. The next morning after mom Isabel went to the farm, one of Sam's sisters, Vivian, and his girl-friend, Felicia's friends, came out in the street and started cursing and swearing about Felicia and Isabel. But She did not go outside to curse with them. She was crying and saying why Isabel got Sam locked up and she never locked up her boyfriend for defiling her. She wanted to kill herself. Thinking her life is over being pregnant as a young girl. And have to raise a baby without a father, no more school for her and becoming a young mother and was feeling hurt by Sam and the way he disowned the pregnancy, behaved and acted towards her, and was feeling so embarrassed of what people would say about her. Felicia did not leave the house for at least 2-3 weeks.

But Felicia was so surprised her friend Cutie was sleeping with Sam also. She thought that she was her friend. And she knew Sam, and I was seeing each other, and she would tell her stuff about them. she trusted her, and she betrayed her

# Episode Four

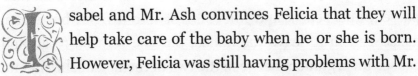

Isabel and Mr. Ash convinces Felicia that they will help take care of the baby when he or she is born. However, Felicia was still having problems with Mr. Ash. One day she overheard her mother and Mr. Ash talking about her pregnancy and how she should get an abortion. But Isabel refused because she thinks everyone knows that she is pregnant now. And she will take care of the baby.

Some months later Mr. Ash asked Felicia if he could help strengthen the baby that she is carrying. She said to him, *'You are so dirty and nasty'*. Rick overheard them in the yard. And came out of the house and said to him that with everything that is going on with her, you want to sleep with her. Rick started to argue with Mr. Ash; he ran to get his dagger, and Rick grabbed two big stones from the ground then threw them after Mr. Ash. Isabel didn't ask what happened. She just listened to Mr. Ash's side of the story, And not her children's. It's like she chose him over her children.

She went into the house and threw out Rick's clothes. Felicia started to cry and said to Isabel. Rick heard him asking me if he could strengthen the baby in my belly. That is what caused the fighting between them. it is not fear you put him out because of this man who wants to sleep with me. But Rick hugged and said to Felicia that it's ok, *'I will go and ask grandfather if I can stay with him for now'.*

Later that day, Rick took his stuff and went to stay with Isabel's adopted dad that lives right above them. Felicia was feeling so tired and stressed out with everything that was happening. And wondering if she is next to get thrown out. Two months passed, and Felicia and Mr. Ash got into a fight, but Isabel asked Felicia to leave the house, but she refused to go and caused an argument between the two of them. Isabel went and got the police to put her out, but Felicia started asking Isabel, what have I done that you want to put me out on the street for this man?" *'You are doing to me the same thing as you did to Rick'.* The police arrived and they said to Isabel, the girl is young and pregnant, where will she go? They beg Isabel for her to stay until the baby is born. However, Isabel said she didn't care where she went.

That same evening, one of the neighbors came to speak with Isabel that Felicia is just 13 years old, and has a big belly in front of her, and will soon be giving birth to her first grandson or granddaughter. Where will she go? Isabel considers and gives her another chance and tells her to stay. When the police officers came to the house, some of the neighbors came out looking at them. Felicia was feeling so ashamed and embarrassed for what Isabel did to her. She wonders which mother will treat her children that way for the sake of a lover. She still wondered why because he pays the bills and buys food in the house. That's why she's always on his side, even if he's wrong. She is afraid he will leave her; that is. why she treats Rick and her like trash over him and his money.

Life didn't get any better for her. She was having evil thoughts; she kept on saying that nobody likes her. One day she was thinking of taking her own life. But then she said to herself that her life will be horrible in hell and worse than what she is going through and that one day everything will be alright. Everyone was staring at her; some people were even talking about her. They were wondering how an innocent girl got pregnant, where her parents were. Mom Isabel probably thinks that she is a disgrace to the family. But she would have to quit school. Because of what her friends would say and laugh at her. Nobody else cares to know what she is going through. She knows that she needs help, but who will she talk to? She was wondering whether I should go live with my dad. But remember, there is a stepmom, and she doesn't like any of her father's children outside hers. And her life might be worse with her dad. Or must she go back to Grandma Mell`s house, so she decided to stay with Mom Isabel and face what she is going through.

# Episode Five

One day, Felicia was home, and her stomach was hurting, so she told Isabel that she was not feeling good. Isabel told her to go and relax. Later that evening, Isabel cooked dinner and called Felicia, but she couldn't eat. The next morning, she woke up not feeling good; therefore, she didn't go anywhere. Isabel told her to go take a shower, and she did just that. And she relaxed throughout the rest of the day. Later in the night, around 9 pm, they all went to bed, but Felicia couldn't sleep. She was having pain in her stomach, so she went and woke Mom Isabel up. It was around 1 am, and she told her that her belly was hurting a lot. Isabel said to her that you are getting contractions and you need to get dressed.

Felicia was so frightened and asked what contractions. Isabel said it is when the baby is ready to be born. Felicia was scared about having the baby. Meanwhile, Isabel called one of the neighbors who had a taxi to take them to the hospital; Felicia was crying so much due to the pain. When they get to the hospital, Mom Isabel takes Her to be registered in the emergency room; the nurse takes her information and takes them to the hospital, where people deliver their babies. The nurse gets her set up with a bed. The pain was unbearable for Felicia, the nurse told her she is going to put an IV drip in her arm, which will hurt a bit.

Isabel waited for her to be settled in. Before leaving, she told her that she would come back later in the evening to check up on her. When Isabel was about to leave, Felicia started to cry and begged her to stay, but she told her she had to go and do something. She tells Felicia that she will be back before the baby is born.

In the evening, Felicia had a baby boy around 6 pm. Everything went well with her and the baby. The baby weighed 5 pounds 5 oz and was tiny. Isabel came back to the hospital. When Isabel entered the room, Felicia asked her why she wasn't here to see the baby born. Isabel replies that she had to do something and that she was sorry. Felicia didn't believe her. She brings her some food to eat. She asks if she can go home now with the baby, but Isabel tells her that she has to wait for the doctor to check her and the baby to make sure everything is ok first before discharging her.

Felicia was feeling sad and scared; she started to cry and didn't want to stay in the hospital because it was creepy and there was no privacy. Isabel said to her that she will be back tomorrow and said good night to Felicia and left. The next morning the doctor came to see Felicia and the baby. She asked him if she was going home today. and he said no because he wanted to run another test on the baby to make sure everything was great. But Felicia was not happy to hear that she had to stay there another day. She was sad all day and Isabel didn't come back to see me today, she said. Felicia was just praying for the next day to go home.

Finally, the doctor passed the ward and told her she and the baby we're going home today. He signed the discharged papers and gave them to the nurse. Felicia was excited and went to a phone booth in the hospital. And she called Isabel and told her that she and the baby were being discharged from the hospital. Isabel says that she was on her way to come and pick them up. Thirty minutes later, she came, and Felicia was so glad to see her. Isabel signed the discharge form and they left the hospital. and went looking for a taxi to take them home, they finally got home.

Felicia knows the journey wasn't easy for her and was happy to be home. The baby was so tiny she couldn't lift him up well. Isabel was always helping her and going to the doctor appointment with them. They named the baby Max. One day, Sam wanted to come and see the baby. He sent one of his friends to ask Isabel if he could see the baby. But she refused, *'he must not come anywhere near my daughter and baby max. she will do something to him that he will not like'.* She said that they don't want anything to do with him and his family. He said the baby is not his own; Why does he want to see him now? Isabel tells his friend to tell Sam, she is now the baby's grandmother and father, and she will take care of him and her daughter.

Sam was not happy about what mom Isabel told his friend to tell him. He came begging her that he was sorry because his girlfriend and his mother were the ones encouraging him to say he never had an intercourse with her daughter and the baby is not his own. Sam told Isabel that he is sorry for everything that happened and should forgive him for putting Felicia through that. Isabel told him that she won't forgive him for what her daughter going through and suffer for the past nine months and doesn't want to contact her and that little boy ever. Sam insisted that the baby is his, and she cannot stop him from seeing him.

Sam walked out of the yard and went his way, upset and mad. Isabel told Felicia that Sam came begging her to see baby Max, but she told him to stay away from you and the baby. She told mom Isabel that he is the baby's father, how can you keep him away from his baby. Isabel told Felicia, *'let me tell you something. If you ever let that fool anywhere near that little boy, I will put you out of my house on the street to go and meet him'*. He and his mother are evil and wicked people. *His mother never encouraged him to take care of his responsibility as a young man. Instead, she carried him to be baptized, looked at what he is still doing, and wants people to believe they are Christian. Just listen to me and stay away from that boy; you and the baby will be okay.*

The baby was very sick at three months, with a fever and crying a lot. They try all ways by giving him some medicine and rubbing him down to stop the fever. But nothing is working. The next morning Isabel told Felicia that they had to take the baby to the hospital. They took him to the doctor, and she checked him out and said he was doing fine. It's just a fever, and she gave them some medication for the fever. And they went back home with the baby and gave him some of the medicine the doctor gave to them. The baby was crying and was vomiting up everything he ate.

Felicia started to cry and asked her mother what was happening to her baby max. Isabel quickly takes up baby max and takes him to her adopted father. Mr. Samurai, who lives right above her house. She went into his house with baby Max and told him that something is wrong with him. He just keeps crying all day. He looked at the baby and said he is mildew by someone who loves him. He takes the baby from Isabel and rests him on the table. He got some soursop leaves and some other stuff, put them under the baby, and lit a fire with some brushes in a little bowl, and held it over the baby. He was crying a lot. Mr. Samurai took up the baby and put him on his lap and anointed him with some oil.

It takes him like an hour and a half to do everything. The baby was okay after everything. She was happy that her baby Max was doing just fine again. Max was now one and a half years old, and Felicia was about 15 years old now. She couldn't take care of the baby by herself. So, Isabel is taking care of the baby; Felicia thinks of doing something with her life. She decided to go to evening classes. She can meet new people, and develop new skills, and to pick up where she left off in her education. She was still battling with Mr. Ash and everyone around her. Although she had baby max, she was still not happy and never felt wanted by her family. Felicia started to hang out with some friends from classes and came home late, but Isabel didn't like it and confronted her to come home to help take care of her child. But she didn't not like what Isabel was telling her. She told her, why do you care what I am doing now?" Isabel said to her I always love you and want what is right for you. Felicia said stop right there, with tears in her eyes, because if you do, why give me away, your only daughter, to a woman you never knew, and leave me to get abused by your so-called boyfriends.

And look at me at this young age, 15 and already a mother. If you did have love for me and take care of me. I am sure my life will be good as a young lady. You even take Dex at age 3 and give him to his dad, and his wife. We don't even know him and I'm sure he doesn't even remember his siblings. Isabel told her that was in the past and she needed to move on and let go of what had happened. And she was very sorry that she had to go through that in life. Felicia tells her it's easy for her to say because you have never gone through it.

# Episode Six

～

elicia continues to live her life. One night, a church service took place at the roadside not too far from where she lived. She decided to take a walk down there to listen. On the 6th night, there was an alter call, and the Pastor said, *'if anyone here doesn't know the Lord as his personal Savior and would like to know him come'*. Felicia said to herself that if she gives her life to Christ and lives for Him, her life will change, and things will get better for her. So that night, she stepped up to the altar and gave her life to God. They prayed with her and asked her for her contact address.

Felicia started to go to church but wasn't ready to get baptized. She continued her normal life, such as hanging out with her friends and going out with them. When she turned 16 years old, she told her friends that Mom Isabel now wants to be a mother to her. when she is already a mother like her. When she was supposed to, she didn't, and it was too late for her. Felicia will go home late sometimes and act like she didn't care if she was locked outside. Sometimes she will sleep on the porch when she gets home late.

She feels like something was still missing in her life and why she was still not happy. a guy who was working on a house next door, and Felicia went over to talk to him. His name was Edward, and they became friends. One day Edward asked Felicia out on a date, and she was excited and said yes to him; they went to the movies. After that, they started to go out more and fell in love with each other. Then she invited him home to mom Isabel and Mr. Ash, but Mr. Ash didn't not seem to like him, but mom Isabel did and welcomed him to the house.

Edward starts taking care of Felicia and her son Max like his own child. He was a very nice person but was a jealous guy. Edward's older brother was getting married, and he invited her to go with him and meet his family though she had met some of his family members before. She left Max home with mom Isabel. They went for the weekend to Edward's brother's house. She met his mom, his two sisters, his brothers, the stepdad, and the sister-in-law. He introduced her to them. His mom said to Felicia, *'nice to meet you, and hugged her'. Did* She reply, thank you? She enjoyed the weekend with Edward and his family. They came back home.

One day, Felicia went to the shop to buy some food. And was stopped by one of Edward's male friends to ask for someone. At the same time, Edward was passing by the street and saw the two talking and passed them straight without saying hello to his friend. Felicia excused herself and hurried to catch up with Edward. She finally did and asked him what's wrong with him and whether he didn't see her talking to her friend. He stopped and was demanding for her to tell him what they were talking about. She told him that he should find out for himself, when you passed us on the street. And he told her I didn't want you talking to none of my friends around here. Felicia replies, why not. Are you jealous that your friend will take me away from you? He did not say anything back to her.

The relationship between them was going great until one Sunday night. Felicia went to church. It was Mother's Day that Sunday, and the church was celebrating it. They asked who was the youngest mother in the church, so someone shouted out, *Felicia*. She gets a call up to collect a prize for being the youngest mother. When the church was over, she walked up with some friends from church, going the same way. They stopped and began talking about how they can't believe Felicia was the youngest mother in the church.

As they were still there, Edward passed by them and he greeted the gentleman standing there with Felicia and the lady. He was one of Edward's friends; he didn't say anything else but continued walking up the street. Then Felicia said goodnight to her friends and left. She meets up with Edward on her way home. He stopped her, grabbed her hand, and asked her what she and the guy were talking about. She explained that it was more of a group with the lady; they couldn't believe she was the youngest mother in the church. Edward didn't believe and slapped her because he didn't want her to be talking to them. She started fighting with him and was crying and telling him to let her go. He finally let her go, and she went home and told Mom Isabel and Mr. Ash what happened. Mom Isabel asked why he hit her. Felicia told them to tell him that she didn't want anything to do with him, and it's over between the two of them.

Mr. Ash was not pleased with Edward slapping Felicia and said he put his hands and hit you. When I see him, I will let him know not to put his hands on you again. Edward didn't come to the house that night. He came to the house a few days after all the drama. Felicia was on the porch with Max and Isabel. Edward greeted them with a good evening, but Felicia didn't answer him, and she went into the house. Mom Isabel asked him why he slapped her the other night, when she was coming from church. He said he saw her talking to this guy and he didn't like it. But mom Isabel asked him if it was just the two of them talking and he responded negatively. Mom Isabel told him, my daughter really loves you, and I know she will never cheat on you with anyone. I see the way she is with you. And you have to stop hitting on her. And he promised her he would never put his hands on her again.

Edward went into the house to talk to Felicia, but she would not speak to him and told him to leave her alone. He holds her hands and says that he is sorry and he will not hit her again. That he loves her and their son. Felicia said to him that when you love someone, you don't hit them or mistreat them. *All I ever do is love you. I will never cheat on you, especially not with your friends.* Felicia gave him another chance and told him, the next time you put your hands on me again, *I will leave you for good, and I meant it.*

The relationship continued between them again, and everything was going well. But Felicia wanted him to stop the life he is living and give his life to God. But Edward told her he is not ready, she asked him why, but he didn't know. Felicia continues to go to church and live for God. Edward had finished building his house and asked her to come and live with him, but she refused. Felicia said to him I can't live with you until you marry me.

Felicia becomes friends with this girl named Jazz, living with her boyfriend and his family in the blue house right below her. Jazz has a little girl and is pregnant with another. But her boyfriend will always beat her. Felicia will feel sorry for her and one day asked her why she allows her boyfriend to beat her continually and don't do anything about it. Her mother always comes up and curses him and will not go with her, and then she stays with him. Jazz said it was because of the children. Felicia said she thinks she loves him but that love will kill her someday.

Mom Isabel told Felicia to keep away from that Jazz. Mom Isabel does not like her and will warn Felicia to stay away from her. But she didn't, she took her son's small clothing and gave them to Jazz for her baby. Edward built his house close to where his mom lives. But Felicia will not go to the house. Jazz had the baby, and it was a boy; a couple of months later, Edward came over to Felicia's house and told her that Jazz came to his house asking him for money to buy stuff for her children, and he gave her. but it's more than one time. But you never said anything about it before, so why do you feel like telling me now?" Edward said she even offers herself to him. But he told her that he was in love with Felicia. Felicia shouted surprisingly, *Are you kidding me?"*

One evening, Jazz acts in an unusual manner to Felicia. Felicia was at the side of the road next to her house fetching water in a bucket, when jazz came and pushed Felicia's bucket over, and puts her bucket under the pipe, so Felicia pulls her from the pipe. Both of them started to fight each other. Everyone came out and tried to separate them from fighting. Jazz started to curse Felicia and left to get her mother and bring her to fight Felicia and Mom Isabel. But they weren't successful.

Jazz and her mom were on the roadway, cursing and carrying on about what they will do to Felicia when they meet her anywhere. But Jazz takes Felicia to court about the fighting they have. But when the judge found out what happened the day of the fight, she placed both of them under six months probation and if they break it she would send them to jail for one year. But after that, whenever Jazz's mom met Felicia anywhere, she would try to fight with her, but she was never successful.

Six months later, Felicia and Edward were still in a relationship. Felicia told Edward she was going to get baptized, and she wanted to be fully committed to God and church. And there will be some conditions between both of them now. She can't live and do the things she used to live her life with until he married her. Edward agreed and decided to wait with her on that because he loved her.

One Saturday evening, Felicia went to the city for mom Isabel to get her some medication. And was on her way back home, but she decided to stop off down the road and walk-up. On her way, she stops at a shop where Edward goes every weekend to gamble his money. Felicia had one of her little cousins with her. And she said to her to go to the shop and call Edward for me. But his response to the cousin tells her I am coming. Felicia was by the roadside about 20 minutes waiting for Edward, when Sam, the father of her son, passed by and asked how his son was doing. She was telling Sam when Edward came up and saw them talking.

Sam left and went his way. Edward gets upset, grabs Felicia by her hand, and asks what she and Sam were talking about. And she told him why when I called you didn't come, so if you wanted to know what we were talking about since i sent and called you. But Edward didn't like it and slapped Felicia in her face, and she told him to let her go because he was hurting her and get him to let her hands go. She ran up the street to her house and told Mom Isabel what had happened. But mom Isabel was happy about what happened to Felicia, because she didn't like Sam for what he did.

Felicia was mad and upset with Edward and Mom Isabel for what he did to her. You chose his side for hitting me because of money and because it was Sam I was talking to this time. I *know you never loved and cared about me and what happened to me. But this time, I am finished with Edward for good. And nothing or anyone will say to me will not make me stay in this relationship for my death.* Felicia ranted. Felicia told mom Isabel that she should tell Edward to stay away from her, and it is really over between the two of them.

The next two days, Mom Isabel went to the farm, and Mr. Ash went to work. Felicia and her son were home when Edward showed up and begged her that he was sorry for hitting her again. But she replied to him, it's over between them, this time for real. He thinks she was joking about it this time, but she was not. She told him she was so tired of him beating her like she is a nobody, and she went through too much in her life to continue like this with him. He continues to hold on and tells her he is sorry. Felicia said she doesn't want to live the rest of her life that way, considering what she went through in the past.

Also, she doesn't want to spend the rest of her life with someone who doesn't trust her and beats her too. He held on to her, and she held onto his jersey, and it got ripped, and he pushed her against the wall, and her son was crying, so he let her go and left the house. She told him if he ever came back around her, she would call the police and have him arrested. He went on the line with her clothing hanging and ripped one of her dresses. And said to her, you will regret this, and went his way. When Mom Isabel came home, Felicia told her what happened to her and Edward. And it is over between them both this time. I know you love him but my life is more important to me than money. And she wants to live to see her son grow up.

# Episode Seven

ne year later, after leaving Edward, Felicia stopped going to church and started living a careless life doing what she thinks please her. That's when she starts going to clubs and drinking with her friends. She even falls in love with a man whose name is Wayne that could be her father. He always comes to a shop down the street close to Felicia's house almost every evening. And she will leave home and go away with Wayne in his vehicle to go and have fun with him. He will always give her everything she wants.

Mom Isabel never liked the man, the two of them dated for a while, until one Sunday night, Felicia went out with her uncle and his girlfriend to a party in the city. After the party, Felicia's uncle and one of his friends requested that Felicia and his girlfriend go for a walk at the Fort. They all went for a walk when the uncle's friend tried to force himself on Felicia, but she kicked him and ran off. The uncle asked her what happened, and she told him that his friend tried to push himself on her. But her uncle didn't believe what his friend did. She cried and went home that night since her uncle didn't believe her.

The next morning Felicia was not feeling well, and went to the doctor and he gave her some medication pills; after the doctors appointment, she went to see one of her girlfriends and told her what her uncle's friend did to her that night. She went home that evening after leaving her friend's house to hear what her uncle and his girlfriend revealed about her to Mom Isabel.

When Felicia gets home, Mom Isabel starts to confront her about what her brother told her about the incident at the Fort. Mom Isabel didn't believe her side of the story but believed the uncle's side of the story that she forced herself on the man. Mom Isabel told her to take her things and leave her house. She ran off to meet Wayne, hoping he would believe her, but he didn't believe her either and believed her uncle's lies. Wayne told her the relationship between them was over, and he doesn't want to be with a little whore like her anymore.

Felicia left crying, and went back home, took her son, hugged him, and kissed him with tears in her eyes. She also told him she loves him and is very sorry for what she is about to do. She put her son at the back door of Mom Isabel's house and left her things at the back of the house. She grabs the pills she got from the doctor and goes by the neighbor's gate, and sits down crying, asking God why did she come into this world to suffer like this, that she is tired of living in so much pain where she is not welcomed by her own family, who don't care about her and love her. She takes the bag with the pills and takes half of it. One of Felicia 's cousins saw her taking the pills, ran over to her, and took the bag with the pills from her. But she had already taken half of it. The cousin called mom Isabel, but she said she would stay there and die.

Then Felicia got up and walked down the road near to where Wayne was at the shop. Minutes later, she fainted to the ground and was there for a while; She was frosted from her mouth; Felicia's cousin came looking for her, saw her on the ground, and called for help. And the people there were begging Wayne to come and take her to the hospital, and He said he is not taking her, so the gentleman that owns the shop asked him if she was one of your sisters or daughters, would you like anyone to treat them like that. He eventually came and helped lift her up and put her in the van, and took her to the hospital, where they rushed her to the emergency room quickly. The doctor attended to her; he asked the name of the pills she took. Someone who came with her had the bag with the pills and gave it to the doctor.

Felicia was not responding; he quickly pushed a tube into her nose down to her throat and ran IV in her hand. She looked like she was dead where he had to poison her over again for her to stay alive. The doctor told them she would have died if she were not brought in for the next ten minutes. She started to vomit up everything from her stomach. Her body was dehydrated and weak.

Felicia stayed in the hospital for three days, no one came to see her in the hospital. She was okay and discharged. Felicia called one of her girlfriends that day and asked her if she could stay with her for a week or two. She told her to come, and she took a van and went to her friend's house. The friend hugged her and asked her what she's thinking of trying to take her own life, that she loved her, and Felicia started to cry and said that she was sorry for what she did. And that she always felt like an outcast in her family. Her friend asked her what she planning to do now with her life. Felicia said she didn't know yet. But she is not going back to Mom Isabel's house. After two weeks, She left her friend's house and went back to Mom Isabel's house to get her clothing and see her son. When she got here. Mr. Ash was home with Max. Felicia greeted him, and when Max saw her, he ran and hugged her. She started to cry and said to him that she loved him and was sorry for everything. Mr. Ash asked her where she was staying, she replied that she didn't have anywhere to go now. Felicia was at the house when Mom Isabel got home from the farm, and asked her what she was doing here in her yard. Felicia replies that she came to get her things and see Max. Mr. Ash calls Mom Isabel in the house and tells her to take Felicia back home because she doesn't have any way to stay. And look at her; she needs to be with her family. Mom Isabel and Mr. Ash came out of the house and told her she can stay with them. Felicia thanked both of them for letting her stay here again. She promised to try her best to do good and help out around the house and with her son.

# Episode Eight

&

As time passed by, Felicia will go to the farm with Mom Isabel and even with her cousins in the evenings. She will even go to the city market to sell vegetables for Mom Isabel from the farm. Felicia was happy again and started to go back to church, give her life back to Christ, and get baptized this time. She was even going back to the evening classes. And chilling with her friends from church and her cousins.

Felicia met this young lady with a baby girl by the roadside. She said to the young lady that her baby is so cute, and the young lady replied, *thank you*. Felicia asked her what her name was and the baby also, she said her name is Miranda and my baby's name is Iyesha. Felicia asked her how old she was, and she answered that she was 12 years old. Felicia replies to her, *'hmmm, welcome to my world'*. She takes the baby from her, and she explains everything that happened to Felicia and what she went through as a young girl. Felicia asked her, so, where is your mom? Miranda said she lives by the house next to the church where you attend, but she always drinks and smokes.

Felicia was touched by Miranda's story, and told her about what she Felicia went through and she has a son called Max. Miranda asked Felicia if she wanted to be the baby's Godmother, and she said yes to her. Three weeks later, the baby was christened at the same church Felicia goes to down the street. Miranda gets involved with a young man a couple of blocks away from Felicia's house, Miranda becomes pregnant again with a little boy. Felicia will go at times and get Iyesha to spend the weekend with her. Mom Isabel and Mr. Ash were ok with Felicia bringing her to the house at times.

When Felicia went to get Iyesha, her Mother Miranda asked Felicia if she could stay with her for one week, and she said yes to her. At that time, Iyesha was just two and a half years old. Felicia took Iyesha and went back home. one week, Felicia went to take back Iyesha to her mom, but the young man said she left three days ago. he doesn't know where she went, she even left the baby with him; Felicia asked if she can leave Iyesha with him, and he said no; she said okay to him and left to go to Miranda's mom. where she was living close to the church. When Felicia got to the house, Miranda's mom was there. She asks her, where is your daughter? She said she didn't know where Miranda was.

Felicia wanted to know what happened to her and also wanted to give Iyesha back to her mother. She is nowhere to be found, and her son's father said he doesn't know where she went. Felicia asked the grandmother what to do with her grandchild now that Miranda was nowhere to be found. Miranda's mom told her that she couldn't take baby Iyesha and she even struggled to take care of her children.

Felicia was wondering what Mom Isabel and Mr. Ash would say if she took Iyesha back to the house. She took her back to the house and explained to Isabel that she couldn't find Miranda and nobody knows where her whereabouts are. When Mr. Ash came from work, Mom Isabel talked to him about what happened, and he said it was okay to let her stay until her mother comes back for her.

Three years passed by, and Miranda didn't come and look for her children. Everyone loves the little girl so much Felicia will even treat her as her own child. Felicia was working to take care of an olderly woman, she will take care of herself and her son and Iyesha with the money she gets from her salary. Mom Isabel will help her out sometimes. It was time for Iyesha to go to school; Felicia got everything she needed for school; she took her to get her four-year-old Vaccination shot at the clinic. Felicia makes sure that her son Max and Iyesha have everything they need to go to school.

One day Mom Isabella and Mr. Ash were planning to get married because they started to go to church and decided they wanted to live a good life and serve the lord. That happened for a while with Mr. Ash; it didn't take him long to go back to his wicked ways and started to drink again. One night he left for work; the morning before he came home, he went to the rum shop and got drunk before returning home. That morning Mom Isabella had already left for the farm. When Mr. Ash got home that morning, Felicia and the children were home. But Mr. Ash told Felicia that he didn't want Iyesha to stay in his house. Because she keeps urinating on the bed every night, Felicia then tells him that she doesn't know where Iyesha's mother was and that she had nowhere else for her to go. Mr. Ash started to argue with Felicia and said that is not his problem. She must leave this house today. Mr. Ash then went and got his cutlass after Felicia, her back was turned as he fired a chop with the cutlass to hit her, but Felicia's son saw and pushed his mom out of the way. If it wasn't for your son, he would chop her in the back of her head or kill her that day. After that, Felicia yelled at him, *foolish man, if that cutlass did hit me today you would have been a dead man, you remember what Rick told you before you make him have to leave this house.* And my mother will not marry you. You can go and kill yourself now. That day Felicia got dressed. She also dressed Iyesha and went to the city to go to the Children Aids Society to get help for Iyesha. She met with Miss Daisy and told her what happened, and she needed help for Iyesha. Miss Daisy told Felicia what they could do to help her. She must go and find a place to rent her and Iyesha, and they will give 225 a month for her to take care of Iyesha. Felicia went back to the house with Iyesha, and Mom Isabel was home when she got there. She asked Felicia what happened here today with you and Mr. Ash. Felicia told her what happened and that he nearly chopped her with his cutlass in her back, thanks to her son, so Mom Isabel and Mr. Ash started to curse and said he didn't want Iyesha in his house. Mom Isabel told him she is not going anywhere. She is just a child.

They settled for the night. Felicia went looking for a place to rent mostly every day but couldn't find anything around to rent. As months go on, Felicia gives up looking and continues living at Mom Isabel's house with Iyesha. But sometimes, Felicia will sleep by her friend's house most of the night. She will come to the house in the morning to get Max and Iyesha ready for school. So, this one morning, Felicia decided to take Iyesha to the doctor for the peeing problem; she explained what was happening to her. He said it is normal in children at her age. And with time, it will go away.

Two months later, Mom Isabel and Mr. Ash are having problems. She found out that he is cheating on her with a lady in the same neighborhood just below her house. Mom Isabel called off the wedding. But Mr. Ash didn't like that; this one particular morning, Mom Isabel had left for the farm as usual. Felicia came down from her friend's house to get the children ready for school. Iyesha urinated on her bed that night, so Felicia took the wet bedding and was at the sink washing them when Mr. Ash returned home from work that morning. He looked like he was drinking before he came home. He sounds somehow; Max said to him, dada, you reach home, he replied to max, *yes, my boy.* And he looked at Iyesha and said, "You're leaving this house today for real this time. She started to cry, and Felicia said she is not going anywhere. Felicia asked him what his problem with this child is, she is just a little girl. *'Is it her fault she urinates on her bed? Maybe the poor girl is afraid; your mouth has no respect for anyone in this house,' asked Felicia to Mr. Ash.* Felicia told Nick to take Max to school and left Iyesha. Felicia told him that her mother doesn't want to marry him anymore, which is killing him. Felicia said that the only thing left for you to do is run away, drink poison and die, saying those things made Mr. Ash even madder than before. He then told Felicia to get out of the house and he threw everythings out of the house. Mr. Ash was putting on a show for the people and the neighbors to watch.

Felicia went and got ready and took Iyesha and went back to the children's aid society to see Miss Daisy. She didn't have any way to keep Iyesha that her stepfather threw her out of the house. And she will have to find a place to put Iyesha. Felicia was not happy to do this, but she wanted a good and better life for Iyesha. Felicia didn't want her to live a life like her, she wanted her to get a good family who would take good care of her and give her all the things she cannot give her. Miss Daisy was looking for someone that Iyesha can stay with. Felicia was with her and told her she was going to live with some new people, and she would be ok. With tears in her eyes, she was just six years old. She hugged and kissed her and said I wish my life was different and I had my own place to take good care of you myself. Iyesha told her, why are you crying? She asked because I am going to miss you. Felicia was eating up inside to let her go. The last thing Felicia told her is that she loved her so much and she will always remember her and leave in tears. After Felicia left, she didn't go straight home, she stayed off down by the football field to watch the soccer game. One of her friends told her that her stepfather is in the hospital, so she asked what happened to him; her friend said he went and drank poison after leaving this morning, and the ambulance came and took him to the hospital.

Felicia left and went home. Mom Isabel was home and told her what happened. Mom Isabel was not happy when she got home. everything was thrown outside the house. Max asked where Iyesha is? Felicia told him with some people, and he asked if she was coming back home. Felicia didn't say anything to him but left and went up to her friend's house. He was making fun of Felicia because she made her stepfather drink poison, so she told him it's not funny. Did I hold his head and pure it down his throat?

Please stop, she replied to him. I am so sad I didn't not eat for the day. That man makes me have to give up that little girl to the children Aids society. That man wants everyone to be miserable, just like him. Felicia started to cry, her friend said Iyesha will be ok. They will find her a good home. I hope so, she said. Felicia didn't sleep that night. She was thinking about Iyesha and crying. She remembers what happened to her when mom Isabel gives her away. Felicia saw Mom Isabel with a ring on her finger and asked her, did you go and marry that man in the hospital, despite everything he did. I even heard his sister come to the hospital and curse you too. Felicia told Mom Isabel but you promised us that you would leave him. When Mr. Ash came out of the hospital, Mom Isabel took him back to the house. Felicia decided she couldn't live in the same house with him and went and asked her next-door neighbor, uncle Bee, if she could stay there with him and his grandchildren. Felicia takes her things and moves to her neighbor's house to live. Felicia went back to the children's Aids society to see Mr Daisy about Iyesha, she wants her back. She has found a place to live, But Miss Daisy said she has found a home with a new family and she is very sorry. Felicia asked if she can get the people she is staying with contact numbers, so she can call her sometime. She said the family doesn't want anyone from her family to have any contact with her. Felicia was heartbroken that she would never see Iyesha again. Felicia hated Mr. Ash for everything that happened to Iyesha.

Felicia left After she could not get back Iyesha. She moved out from Mom Isabel's house, but she left Max to live with Mom Isabel. Felicia went to live at one of the next-door neighbor's houses. She decided that she must get out of this place and restart her life over again. Felicia had a friend from church who moved away to Canada; the two always correspond by mail. Felicia's friend heard what she was going through. one day Felicia went to the post office, and she received a letter from her friend in Canada. When she opened the letter, she started to read it. Her friend asked her if she wanted to come to Canada. Because she can get her job babysitting and she can live with the people, Felicia was wondering where she would get the money to go there. She doesn't have a passport and will have to go and get one. So, she did just that and got it in 14 days. She called her friend in Canada and told her she got the passport, and she didn't get the money yet to buy the ticket. But she will try her best to get it and must give her some time. Felicia asked her boyfriend, but he said he didn't have the money to help her. She said to him, it's ok. She even went and asked some of her friends to lend her the money. But no one seems to have the money to lend to her. She started to pray and asked God to take her away from this place and start a new life for herself, Iyisha and her son Max.

One morning, Felicia said to herself I think I am going to ask Mom Isabel to help me. So that same day, Felicia went over to Mom Isabel's house with the letter that her friend sent her in her hand. Max saw her when she reached in the yard and ran to her and grabbed her hand, and she kissed him on his forehead. Mom Isabel was sitting on the porch. Felicia said good afternoon to her. Mom Isabel asked, what is that in your hand?" She replied to a letter from my friend in Canada. Felicia read the letter to Mom Isabel, and she needed her help to buy a ticket to go to Canada for work.

Mom Isabel asked her how you know that it will work out for her. Felicia told her if she doesn't try, how will we know? Felicia said to her it was worth trying. Mom Isabel asked her when do you want to go. She said as soon as she could get the ticket and the flight. Mom Isabel told her she has some cabbage at the farm, she needs to cut, and you sell them. She can go and pay down on the flight. It happened just as they planned; Mom Isabel got the rest of the money and gave it to Felicia to go and finish paying for the ticket. She has one more week before she leaves for Canada. She got everything she needed. She told her cousin that she was going. The time had come, and Felicia was excited to go; Mom Isabela, Max and two of her of cousin's went to the airport with her that morning, the flight was leaving at 9: o'clock am. It was time for Felicia to say goodbye to everyone. She hugged Mom Isabel and told her she loved them with tears in her eyes. She told Max to listen to Mom Isabel and Mr. Ash and behave himself and left to go on the plane. She went on the plane and sat down. After ten minutes the plane left in the air, she was a bit frightened. But her mind was on her son and Iyesha; she left them behind. But she promised if things worked out for her, she would send for them one day to come. With this hope, Felicia travelled to Canada to make her life better.

# Episode Nine

❦

Felicia reached the airport safely and she passed through immigration with a few questions. But was a bit scared, she was waiting for her friend to come to pick her up. She paused and waited but could not see any trace of her in the waiting area. Unfortunately, she did not have her friend's address. her friend Rose got to the airport two hours earlier, thinking that was the time for the flight. Rose had to get back to work, so she left. Rose told herself that she would come back to the airport as soon as she closed. she guessed that Felicia's flight was delayed. Fortunately for Felicia, since she has stepped onto a strange country and doesn't know her whereabouts, she was convinced that the airport was the safest place at that time. She got to the Arrival, took a seat, and was waiting, hungry and scared of what will happen next. She began to think whether or not what mom Isabel said about the journey being risky was true. A lot of fears ran through her head at that time since she was scared. Sitting beside her was a young man who was waiting for his sister to return from Africa. The young man named Lucas realized the fears in Felicia's eyes and actions. He tried to engage her in a conversation to ease her up. She began chatting with him as if she knew him for a long time. They had a long discourse until he saw his sister coming from the terminal. He went to her and hugged her, then introduced her to Felicia as his new found friend.

Lucas wanted Felicia to go with them to contact her friend Rose when she settles. Felicia told him she would wait for her and was convinced she would come and get her. The idea to call Rose with Lucas's phone came up. Lucas called Rose on behalf of Felicia. Felicia spoke to Rose and told her that she had arrived and was waiting for her at the Airport. Rose asked for permission from her supervisor, and she came back to the Airport. Felicia saw her drop her bags and ran and hugged her friend, Rose. She was excited to see her. When Felicia saw her, tears began to drop from her eyes. Rose asked her why she was crying, and she told her that she felt she was missing and alone on someone's land, and she was terrified. since she left home and came to Canada. They take a taxi to Rose's place. Rose took her home, told Felicia to settle down properly before they talk about the next step. After Felicia had washed down, Rose prepared something sumptuous for her to eat since she realized she was famished from the Airport. At the table, Rose asked her about her trip, and they conversed a long time about her life with her mother and everything that has happened to her. Felicia spoke to Rose about all that happened since she had left home, Throughout the conversation, was that she didn't officially break it off with her boyfriend before she came to Canada, After the conversation, rose promised to help her get on her feet to send some remittance for the upkeep of her son, Max, since he was already attending school. After catching up with life. It was cold that night. Rose told her they have to wake up early to take the train and then the bus to her job. So, they went to bed and woke up at 4:30 am; they both got ready and headed out to catch the train. On the train, it was packed with so many people. Felicia couldn't believe what she saw, just as in the movies. They got off the train, went upstairs, and caught a bus to where Rose was taking Felicia to meet the woman she was going to work with. Rose calls the lady, and she meets them at the bus stop. She greeted the lady and introduced Felicia to her, and they talked. She completed her incoming boss, and they had a great relationship to begin with. The boss seemed friendly and accommodating. However, not all that glitters is gold.

Felicia agreed to start immediately. She got the opportunity to talk to Max, and he seemed to be doing well with Mom Isabel. Rose told Felicia she would see her on the weekend and left. Felicia put her bags in the lady's car and they left to go to her house. Felicia was a bit nervous when they got to the house. She took her stuff and went into the house with the lady. She took Felicia to the basement and told her this is where she is going to stay. Then she takes Felicia upstairs and shows her around the house, and introduces her to her five children and their names. That same day the lady showed Felicia what she had to do and how much she would pay her every two weeks. Felicia started to work that day. The husband came home, and the wife introduced him to Felicia.

Felicia started work as a live-in babysitter at the residence of the Lloyds. She wakes up early in the morning to set herself up and take care of their baby, including feeding and changing their nightgown. They also have a little girl who attends preschool and three other older children. At the first start, since the little girl was not familiar with Felicia, she didn't get along with her. This made Felicia's work difficult. She gave Felicia a lot of tough times and always put her into trouble with the mom. This made Mrs. Lloyd not happy with Felicia's work. Felicia tried her best to be a good nanny to her, but she never listened to Felicia. Felicia was worried about the little girl's behavior and hoped it didn't affect her job, seeing it is her first job in Canada and there was no possibility of her getting another job. Felicia was not enjoying the work, and the husband will come home. If they are watching television, he will just take the remote and change the television station without saying anything. Felicia doesn't like her husband. The lady and her husband went away for the weekend. And the husband's parents came to stay with the children and Felicia. On Saturday, Felicia went to see Rose and to collect the rest of her stuff. She told Rose she doesn't like the people, and the husband does not have any manners. Rose told her to get over them, and everything will be fine. Rose directed her to get back to the house, but Felicia didn't know how to get back independently. She came out of the subway and was there sitting on the wall like someone who is lost. Then, a gentleman asked her if she was lost and didn't know where she was going. Felicia told the man she was lost and didn't know where she was going. He asked her if she got a phone number where she was staying and gave it to him. The man then calls the number and talks to the lady. And she gave him the address. The man gave Felicia a ride to the house, the both of them started to talk, and he gave her his number and said if anything was to happen to her, she must call him. She finally reached and thanked him very much for the ride and was happy she got back safe. Back at home, Felicia was determined to win the affection of the little girl, Amanda.

Felicia loved kids, and above all, she was a mother. One day, she decided to go to the playground to spend time with Amanda along with her baby brother. On their way to the park, Felicia held her hand to cross over the street, Felicia told her that they will have fun at the park. Amanda finally agreed, and they went to the park, Felicia asked her what she wanted to do first. She said go on the swing, So Felicia put the stroller with the baby by the side. She then put Amanda on the Swing and started to push her. Then she went on the slide. Then Felicia was seated watching her from where she was sitting with the baby, Amanda climbed up on the bar, Felicia called and ran over to her and told her to get down. She then let go and hurt her head. It was bleeding. Felicia told her but I told you not to climb up here on that bar. She told her let me get you home. Felicia knew she was going to get in trouble with Mrs Lloyds. When they reached back to the house, Amanda ran to her mom crying and told her Felicia pushed her and she hit her head. Felicia could not believe what she was hearing from that little girl mourh. Felicia told Mrs Lloyds what happened, but she looked like she didn't believe her and told her next time you have to watch her carefully in the park. She went to her room. Felicia wondered when she would have a smooth ride in this life. She asked God questions and decided something must work out for her. since, according to Felicia, that is her only escape in life. She called Rose and told her what happened, and Rose encouraged her to take it to the Lord in prayers. Later that evening, Felicia called her mother so that she could talk to Max. Mom Isabel told her that Max wasn't feeling well and they had just returned from the hospital. This news got Felicia very disturbed and felt like going back to take care of Max herself. But Mom Isabel encouraged her that Max will be fine, and should not be too worried. and that it is normal for children to fall sick once in a while. Felicia hung up but could not sleep well that night. She was worried throughout and frightened about her son's health. She decided to go on her knees to pray that God should heal her son. The following morning, Felicia apologized again to Mrs. Lloyd for the previous day's incident. She assured her again that it won't happen again. The job is essential to her and her family back home. Mrs. Lloyd encouraged her to do better and be better at what she is being tasked to do. She later went to the kid's room. To the shock of her life, Amanda jumped out of her bed and hugged Felicia so hard, and thanked her for taking her to the playground. She told Felicia that she was sorry for making up a story about her. She said that because her mother was always working, all the previous nannies were never affectionate, which made her dislike any nanny her mother brought home. Felicia was happy that she was able to win the affection of Amanda with time. They had happy times together. They play at home, and she cooks for them. Amanda started kinder-garten, so Felicia takes her to school and gives her all the motherly love she needs. Felicia told Amanda that she has a son back at home, and he is called Max and tells her that Max is a good and handsome boy just like Amanda is. Mrs. Lloyd realized that Felicia had won the affection of Amanda. Felicia would tuck the children to bed and read them bedtime stories until they fell asleep. So, when Mrs. Lloyd returns from work, the children are asleep, and she cannot even talk to them. Mrs. Lloyd came home early one day, even when she got home, the kids were asleep. Suddenly, she got furious at Felicia and told her not to let the kids sleep that early again and that she wants to bond with her kids. Felicia obeyed. Since then, her boss became picky about everything that Felicia did. Felicia wasn't happy working there any longer. She went down on her knees to pray to God because, for once in her life, Felicia got fed up over time. Felicia went to the lady and told her she was not happy with them, and she must drop her off where she picked her up. That night Felicia called Rose and told her what happened, but Rose said she didn't have any place to stay, and she cannot help her. Felicia said it's okay and hung up the phone. The next day when the lady was taking her children to school, she dropped off Felicia at a bus stop with her stuff. Felicia remembered the guy who brought her home when she got lost. Gave her his contact number and she called him. But the phone rings out, and she leaves him a message. After she didn't get the guy, she went to a nearby hair salon and asked if she could stay there until she got picked up. She told the owner she could help out because she can do hair. Felicia was there until the shop was closed for the day. She went back to the phone booth, called the guy again, and left another message telling him where she was. It was cold out there, and she was afraid and scared. She didn't even have a jacket; she was wearing a jeans sweater. The Place begins to get dark, and Felicia goes to the bus stop shed; every police car and fire stuck she sees will get her frightened. Later, around 9:30 pm, she heard a car horn blow while she was in the bus shed waiting. It was the guy, and she went in the car. He apologized and explained to her that he just finished work, and they went to his house. Where he and his mother live. After a week, Felicia bought a newspaper and looked for another job, where she found one as a housekeeper and was living-in. She spent four months there. She met a woman from the same country where she came from and went to stay with her for two weeks, and she got another job to babysit three children. One day Felicia met this guy named Ray when she was going to the mall. They exchanged phone numbers, and they became friends. On weekends, when Felicia gets her time off from work, she meets up with Ray and goes out with him. He even takes her to his mom's house. Six months later, Felicia found out she was three months pregnant. She didn't have papers. She told him she was pregnant, and he told her not to call back his phone. Felicia told the lady that she is working for and told her what Ray had told her. The lady asked Felicia for his number and called him and told him to be a man to his responsibility, and Ray told Felicia if she kept calling him, he would call immigration on her and make her get sent back where she came from. Felicia tried to lose the pregnancy, but nothing happened. She told Ray's mom and told her she was pregnant, and his mom was happy because she loves Felicia. Two weeks later, the lady Felicia was working to get a phone call from her country. After the call, she told Felicia her husband's niece was coming to babysit the kids, and she would have to find somewhere to go. The following day, Felicia bought a newspaper and found a room where she had to share a kitchen and bathroom up the road not too far from where she was staying. She also found a live-in job to babysit three girls. Felicia's belly had not yet started to show.

# Episode Ten

⟨⟩

After Felicia went to the job and started to work with the Brooke' family takes care of one-year old twin girls and their three-year old sister. The family was very nice, and Felicia loved working with them. Felicia stayed with the family for almost three months before the father lost his job. One day, Mrs. Brooke came to Felicia and told her she had to find another job because she is the only working one and her husband will be home to take care of the kids.

Felicia left and went back to her shared apartment and stayed there for another month. She was late to pick up her check from Mrs. Brooke was two days behind on her rent. When the apartment owner asked for his rent, Felicia told him she didn't get the chance to pick her check, so the man told her he didn't want any more children in his house and that she must find somewhere else to go.

Later Felicia went to her doctor's appointment at the clinic, and she had a sad expression on her face, so the nurse asked her what was wrong, and she told her that she is getting kicked out of her apartment because she can't pay her rent. The nurse told her that she could give her a number for a shelter and call them. After Felicia left the clinic, she went back to her apartment, packed her things, and asked the owner if she could leave her things in the shed; he went outside and told him that she would come back when she found a new place to get them.

That evening Felicia called the shelter and told them that she was coming, and at night she went to the shelter. When she got to the shelter, they registered her and gave her a room that she shared with other women. Felicia was not happy to be there; she was scared and felt alone. She continued to call her baby's father, but he was ignoring her calls. While Felicia was at the shelter, the workers helped her apply for refugee and welfare. An African family was looking for a palace to rent, and they told Felicia that they found a place to rent, and had a basement. Felicia went to check out the palace, and she liked it, so she rented it. After that, Felicia had a baby boy and left the shelter; a week after, she got help moving into her new place. After settling down, Felicia called Mom Isabel back home. She told her that she had a baby boy and a new place. but Mom Isabelle didn't believe her, so one of Felicia's cousins came to visit her, and she called Felicia's family and told them that Felicia had a baby. After six months, one of Felicia's cousins came to live with her for six months. Felicia's cousin got pregnant and went back home, but Felicia convinced her not to go back home, but she left anyway.

After her cousin left, Felicia felt sad and alone. Wes' mom called Felicia to come and visit her and the baby. A few months later, the basement she was living in had become infested with rats, so she complained about it to the landlord, but he didn't do anything. Felicia's baby, Alex, had become ill; he started to cry a lot, and Felicia was worried and called Wes's mom and told her the baby was crying and asked what she should do. Felicia takes Alex to the doctor, the doctor examining him and tells her that she needs to take him to the children's hospital. That even Felicia took Alex to the children's hospital, he was still crying, Felicia was so worried.

The doctors there told her that they needed to run some tests on Alex, so they ran an IV on his hand and admitted him to the hospital. Two days later, when the test came back, they found out that Alex had leukemia and that he would have to stay to get treated for it. So, Felicia told the nurse what was going on in her apartment, so they introduced her to the social worker in the hospital and they talked and gave Felicia a number to call a lady that helps people get housing, so Felicia called the lady and made an appointment to see the lady.

Felicia explained her situation, so the lady helped her find a new place in about two months. Felicia had so much going on for her she moved when Alex was just a year and a month old. In December that same year, Felicia bought a ticket and sent it to her eleven-years old son Max to join her in Canada. The following year, where her lawyer advocated for her to stay in Canada. Felicia had an immigration hearing, she went and got refugee status in Canada. Felicia is happy and thanks the lawyer for standing up for her, and she thanks God Almighty for helping her despite everything she went through.

Felicia had to take Alex to the hospital once every week for his treatment. She also gets max into a school next to her home and Alex into daycare. Felicia was working at an office as an assistant. She went and applied for permanent residence.

Felicia's best friend Jenna came to Canada to visit her and to try and get work. But she was impatient and frustrated. But she spent one month there because of no work, so Jenna went back home. One day, Felicia was going to work when she met a lady that was living in her building at the bus stop. She came up to Felicia and asked her if she does hair braiding. Felicia replied to her, yes, I do. The lady told Felicia her name as Hope.

Hope asked Felicia to do her hair one day. They both caught the bus and went their way. Felicia and Hope became good friends. One day Felicia went to Hope's apartment, and Hope had a friend visiting her from work. She introduced Felicia to her friend Will. Felicia and they became friends and started to date. But they both never told Hope that they were dating, until one day when Felicia told her she was pregnant for her friend Will. he was always there for Felicia and her two sons Max and Alex. Felicia went to the doctor for check-up, and when they checked her blood pressure, it was so high, the doctor admitted her immediately to the hospital. She is only 34 weeks pregnant. Felicia called Hope and told her what happened, and she must help watch the boys for her, please. The doctor introduced labor.

The next day Felicia had a baby boy. But the baby was so small and was not doing well on his own, and he was fed through a tube and spent two weeks in the hospital before getting better. A month later, Felicia brought a plane ticket for Mom Isabel to visit Canada. She gave it to one of her cousins who was going back home for mom Isabel. She came and visited Felicia and her family. Max was happy to see mom Isabel; it's been a while since he left her. She met Will and she didn't like him up that much. She didn't like the place much and wanted to go back home before her time was up. Felicia insisted on her staying, and she missed her farming. Mom Isabel, and Will got along well. Max and Will take her all round. She even met some of Felicia's friends. Her time came for her to go back home and she left.

# Episode Eleven

fter mom Isabel went back home, Felicia continues to live her life with her children and Will. Felicia received her permanent resident card early in the following year. Felicia and Will were planning on getting married. She told her family back home that she and her boyfriend Will are planning to get married. Later that year, Felicia and the boys went to visit Mom Isabel and her family for Christmas. Felicia's friends and family were excited to see her and the boys. Mr Ash was happy to see Max and told him that he had grown very fast. Felicia and the children enjoyed their time with her family and came back home to Canada.

A month later, Felicia was dressing her younger son Jay ready to take him to his doctor's appointment, when she noticed him starting to shake with his eyes rolled back in his head. She called Will from the living room and started to cry. Felicia quickly tells him to call 911, and he was on the phone with the paramedics and told them to turn Jay on his side, and someone is on their way to the house. The paramedics and the firefighters came, and they attended to Jay and asked some questions. They ran an IV on his hand, checked him, and told them they had to take him to the hospital.

Felicia rode with him in the ambulance to the hospital. And Will drove himself behind the ambulance to the hospital. When they got to the hospital, the doctor asked what happened. Felicia told him what had happened, he asked both parents if they have anyone in their family with epilepsy, but both of them said no. The doctor told them he would run some tests on Jay to see what is causing it. Later that day, the doctor admitted Jay to a room on the sixth floor of the hospital.

Two days later, the doctor got back the tests; he said he didn't find anything that was causing the seizures. After one week, Jay was discharged and went home. Three days later, Jay went back to the hospital again. The doctor ran more tests and still couldn't find what was causing the seizures he was having. He was having it very often. Felicia and her friend Hope will take turns at the hospital with him. At times Felicia will cry and ask God to heal her children from their illness. Felicia asks God what she has done to be going through all this, first it was her, and now it is her children. She has so much going on for her with her two younger boys on medication and appointments. Felicia wishes she was with her family back home.

She does what she has to do as a young mother for her boys and makes sure they are doing great despite everything in her life. Felicia continues to work and takes care of her family. She decides that she needs to go and visit her family and plan to go for Christmas with Will and the boys. Felicia's family met Will and they all like him. Felicia and Will talk and agree to get married in her hometown. They enjoyed their visit with Felicia's family, and it was time to go back home to Canada. When they reached the country where to catch the flight back to Canada, there was a problem with Will. When checking in their ticket they asked Will for his document to get back to Canada. He said all he has wass just the ticket and his country passport where he comes from. So, Felicia had to leave him there at the airport and catch the flight with the children. Felicia was confused and wondering why he didn't have his documents, why he went with her, and knowing that he cannot come back to Canada.

On her way back on the plane, Felicia was crying and was not feeling too good about what happened. She wondered what would happen to him if they would send him back to his country of birth or what. When Felicia got home, she got the boys something to eat and got them to bed. She called Hope on the phone crying and told her of what happened to Will at the airport. But Hope told Felicia why he went. If he knew he didn't have the right documents to come back. Felicia said she asked him, and he said he had his permanent resident card.

Felicia didn't hear anything from Will until about five months later when he called from a number that she didn't know. He asked her how she and the boys were doing. She asked him where he was, and he told her that he was at a detention center and didn't know when he would get out. And he will try to come back to Canada. He cut off the phone, and she tried to call back the number he called from, but it was not going.

Felicia suspected something was not right with what he was saying to her. Felicia prayed and asked God whatever was going on with Will to expose the truth. She decided to go to school and learn to be a hairstylist. And she did just so. Max and Alex were going to school and Jay was in daycare. One evening Felicia was by Hope when Will called her cellular phone from a Canadian number. He asked how the boys were doing, and she said they were doing good. Felicia asked Will where he is now, and he replied back home in his country. Hope also spoke to Will and gave the phone back to Felicia; after the call, she decided to call back the number he called from; a lady answered the phone, and Felicia asked if she could talk to Will. The lady said he just left the house and went out. Felicia asked her who is her to him, she said I am his wife; Felicia told her that he promised to marry her and they have a son together and he went to her country with her a couple of months ago. The lady told Felicia that she remembered sometime back. He told her he packed a suitcase and said he was going to a retreat with his church. The lady also told Felicia that both of them married back in their country for 17 years. And she came to Canada and sponsored him to come over, and he has his citizenship for Canada. Felicia couldn't listen anymore and gave the phone to Hope, who was talking to the lady. She even said that she and Will had two daughters and that her husband is a big liar, and she is sorry for all he put her friend through. Hope told the wife that she works together with Will and never knew he was married. The lady asked to see the little boy, but Felicia said no.

She resisted, and Hope said bye and cut off the phone. Felicia started to cry, and Hope hugged her and told her it was okay. She was hurting. She called Mom Isabel and told her what happened. Mom Isabel couldn't believe it. And told Felicia to move on and take care of herself and her children. Felicia continues her study and finishes her hairdressing course, and graduates.

After Felicia school, she started braiding for people and friends at her home and sometimes will go to their house. One day, when Felicia went to pick up her passport, she was walking to go and get the bus. To her surprise, guess who she ran into, Will. She greeted, and she asked him a question. Why did you never tell me that you were married and have two daughters and how he came back to Canada? Will said to her that he never married. She told him you are a liar and a mess. You even came back here and didn't look for me and the boys. And went her way home; Felicia decided that she will never put herself with Will again, and she moved on with her life and her children.

A year later, Felicia's ex-boyfriend from back home contacted her. She asked him where are you, he said in canada. he was visiting his family there. He came to visit her at her place. Felicia always loves him and adores him. During his time in Canada he would sometimes sleep at Felicia's house. And they will go out at times together. Felicia ex-boyfriend time was up, and he went back home to his family. But both of them continue to talk on the phone. Felicia missed her period and took a pregnancy test, and it showed she was pregnant. Felicia always wanted to have his baby before she left home. But now she finally will; Felicia calls him and tells him she is pregnant with his baby and he was happy also.

Despite this, he had a family. Felicia went and did her Ultrasound, and the nurse told her she would have a baby girl. She was pleased because she had three boys already. Felicia called her ex-boyfriend and told him, and he was happy for her also. Felicia had friends who would help her out with the children. And was there for her all the time. Felicia was 36 weeks when she went to her doctor appointment, and her blood pressure was high and was admitted to the hospital.

Later that day, the doctor broke Felicia's water bag and induced the labor. Around 7:30 pm that evening, Felicia got the baby, and she was doing great. Felicia's blood pressure was still a bit high, and they had to get it under control. The next day her blood pressure was back to normal with the medicine they gave her. After spending three days at the hospital, Felicia and the baby were fine and ready to go home. When she took the baby home, Alex asked why she looked so white. Felicia responds to him that she is not white; babies look like that when they are just born. Jay went on the bed and sat down, looking at his baby sister. Felicia named her baby girl, Bebe.

After six months, Felicia went back to work, and Max and Alex were in school, and Jay and Bebe were in daycare. When Bebe was about one and a half years old. Felicia takes one of her girlfriends and the children back to her country to visit mom Isabel and the rest of the family. Everything was going Great; until one morning, Felicia woke up early and went to take her daughter Bebe for a morning stroll down the street. On their way back, Felicia stopped at one of the neighborhood gates and talked to her when she heard a big argument coming from mom Isabel yard. She then went up the road fast with her daughter in her hand. When she reached close to the gate, she handed over the Bebe to one of her cousins when she saw mom Isabel had a dagger in her hand and Mr Ash telling to chop him. Felicia and one family member ran up to mom Isabel and begged her to give them the dagger. Mom Isabel was crying and said she was fed up. Felicia told her I know, but he isn't worth going to jail for.

She told her to look at her grandchildren at the window looking at you, and we came here to spend the holiday with you, not to see you go to jail. Felicia hugged her and told her that she loved her. Mom Isabel was ready to go to the farm. She took her stuff and left for the farm. Mr. Ash was still in the yard and calling her all kinds of names. Felicia told him to calm down and stop because the children and her girlfriend are in the house. She asked him what the matter between you and mom Isabel is. You guys bring out the entire neighborhood and hear the kind of words you use to her in front of everybody. But Mr. Ash did not tell Felicia what caused the problem. He left and went down the road. Felicia gets ready and goes to the city to get some food for the house and the children. When she bounced up on Iyesha's grandmother and one of her aunts in the supermarket. Felicia went over and said hello to them and asked how she was doing. The grandmother replied, "good, Thank you. She told her that Iyesha is staying with her for about two years now. Felicia told her she didn't know that she was staying with you. Because the last time she came back home, she went to visit the lady's house where Iyesha was staying, and she told me she was not home, and every time I called her from Canada, she would tell me she was not around. Iyesha's grandmother said she wanted none of the Iyesha family to visit her and know them. But one day, she found me and brought Iyesha with her belongings and said she can't do this anymore and left without saying a word. She had no choice but to take her. Iyesha's grandmother replied, wow, Felicia told her to tell Iyesha to come and look for her at mom Isabel's house. She then said bye and left to the cashier and went back home. Later that evening, when mom Isabel came home from the farm, Felicia asked her what caused the argument between her and Mr. Ash. She said she asked him about some kind of rope, and he started to curse her. Felicia told her she needs not make him drive her this far. She sees a great mother in Mom Isabel and that she has changed. Felicia hugged her and told her that she loves her very much. Mom Isabel was happy to hear Felicia said she loved her. Iyesha came to visit Felicia one week before she left to go back to Canada. When she saw Iyesha, she ran and hugged and told her that she got so big and missed her so much. And how she was doing, Iyesha told her ok, but Felicia noticed she was not too happy and asked her what was wrong. She told Felicia she went through hell with the lady she was living with and what she put her through. And her grandmother's boyfriend will always come home drunk and will touch her up and will force himself on her. Felicia responds, what? And hugged her and told her that she was very sorry that she went through all of this. And Felicia promised her that when she gets back to Canada, she will buy a ticket and send for her, but it will take some time and she must be patient with her. She spent two days with Felicia and the children before going back to her grandmother's house, and she gave her some money to help out with school and some clothing. Felicia felt so sad that she made her go through all this and was crying and blaming herself. It was time for Felicia, her friend, and the children to return home to Canada.

# Episode Twelve

୬

After Felicia returned from visiting her family, she continued her normal life with her children and friends. A couple of months later, Felicia had a friend named Ann visit her from back home. She also had her boyfriend in Canada, but she stayed half of the time with Felicia and the rest with her boyfriend. Ann wanted to stay, but she couldn't find a job before her time was up. So, she decided she was going back home. So, Felicia bought a ticket and some other things and sent for Iyesha to come to Canada to meet her as she promised her. A month later, Iyesha came to Canada. Max was happy to see her; as time went on, Iyesha settled in and attended school. Some years later, Felicia decided that she would start dating and be ready to meet that special someone. She went online looking for love. After days of searching, a guy sent her a message that caught her attention. Felicia went through his profile page and looked him up. She said to herself that he is not that bad, but he was from an African country. She remembered hearing people talking about not dating or marrying a man from an African country. But Felicia decided to try for herself. So, she replied to the guy, and they started to talk. They introduced themselves and began to chat through social media. They chat almost every day on social media and the phone. According to him, the young man named Tun fell in love with Felicia and told her how he felt about her. She told him about her and her family. As time went on, he invited Felicia to come and visit him in Cairo City, where he was staying within the space of four months. Felicia told her friends about the young man and allowed her friends to communicate with him. She asked her friends what they thought about him. Her friends told her he seemed like a nice person and that he sounded serious about her. Felicia accepted his invitation to go and visit him. She was afraid to go to a strange place like Cairo city to visit a guy she didn't know much about. She then went to a close friend to talk to her about her fears. She advised Felicia to register her name in the database for Canada in case something went wrong or happened to her. Felicia asked one of her friends, Jo, to take care of the children for her. She was just going for two weeks. She got her ticket and went to Cairo city. It took her two days to get there. When Felicia reached Cairo International Airport, she had to buy a visa for 15 US dollars to get through customs. Felicia was a bit scared to be there, but she became nervous about meeting them when she saw the guy and two of his friends. But she told herself that she could do this and get through with it. Felicia went over to where the young men were standing; she hugged her friend and he introduced her to his friends. They welcomed her to Cairo City. She replied, thank you. Felicia was pleased to see her friend with a smile on his face. He took the suitcase from her and put his hand around her neck, and they all walked out of the airport. They took a taxi to his Place. On their way, his two friends who accompanied him to the airport got off and waved goodbye. They finally reached where Tun was living. He opened the door of the apartment, and they went inside. Two other people were staying there with Tun. He introduced Felicia to a young lady. Her name is Fumie and her brother, Fex. They welcomed Felicia as she sat down on the couch. She replied to them with her thanks. Tun got Felicia and himself something to eat then she took a shower. Felicia was so tired from her trip, so she said good night and went to bed. When she woke up the next morning, she asked Tun if she could call her friend, Jo, and her children. He told her after they had breakfast. They dressed and went down the street by the computer shop. Felicia was happy she got to talk to her children and her friend. She was enjoying her stay with Tun, going places with him and his friends. But one day, Felicia and Tun went downtown to Cairo. It was so hot that day, and she wanted to call her children. They went to a small shop to make the call. Felicia was on the phone when her nose started to bleed. She calls Tun and he takes her to the back of the shop and gets water to wash her face. But her nose started to bleed more heavily. They both were scared, and Tun asked Felicia what was happening to her. She replied that she guessed it was perhaps because of the hotness of the weather; she hasn't drank water for the day, and her body is probably overheated. Tun got a towel and water and went behind a shop to wash the blood from her nostrils. He takes Felicia to the hospital close by. Everyone was just looking at them. Nobody seems to speak English there, so they left and went to a pharmacy across the street where Tun got some drugs, cotton, and some other stuff to put on her nose to stop the bleeding. Felicia wanted to go back to the house. They take a taxi back, and Felicia's nose finally stops bleeding. She just takes a shower and relaxes for the rest of the night. Finally, the time was due for Felicia to go back home to her children. Felicia arrived safely in Canada. Her children were excited to see their mother. Felicia called Tun and let him know that she arrived back home safely. He was happy to know that. The relationship between the two continues on the phone and social media with phone calls and video chat. She told her friends all about her trip and her time with Tun. He seems to be a nice guy, and she likes him and he also likes her too. Her friends were happy for her. As time went on, Tun asked Felicia to marry him, and she agreed. She told her friends and family she was going back to Cairo city to marry Tun. They advised her to make sure this is what she wants and what makes her happy. Felicia bought her dress and other stuff to take with her, even the rings. Tun bought her the ticket online for her and her daughter Bebe to come. Felicia and her daughter, Bebe, arrived in Cairo city. Tun was excited to meet Bebe; she was just about to turn two years old. He lifted her up in the airport and carried her to the taxi. Tun lived in a different apartment with two of his friends; a male and female and two bedrooms. Felicia and Tun Stay in the other room. Felicia was excited to see Tun again for the second time and could not believe they would get married in a week. The next day, she called her children back home to let them know that she had arrived safely and made sure they were doing great. Felicia and Tun sit down to talk about the wedding and what will happen. 'They went to the registry to get everything organized and done for the wedding. He applied for a resident permit for Felicia. Everything went well for them. Tun and his friends went and got a hall for the reception. Felicia asked Tun who is coming to the wedding, and he said his friends. Both of them had no family there. Tun made a promise to Felicia that he will love her and her children and will always be there for them. Felicia was happy with him and ready for the marriage. The day came for the wedding, and both were happy. They all got ready and went to the city hall for the marriage ceremony with her daughter and three of his friends. A lady married the two of them. They shared rings and kissed, then signed the book. Then, they all went back to the reception hall. There were a lot of people that Felicia didn't know much about. The wedding party went on, and they took pictures on and on until it was time to leave. The hall is only for a limited time. Felicia and her husband left and went back to his apartment. They changed their wedding clothes, his friends came over, and the party continued from there until late. Everyone left so that the married couple could get some sleep. Two days after the wedding, Tun takes Felicia to the Canadian embassy to try and get a visa to Canada with her and her daughter. Unfortunately, it didn't happen for him. He even took her to the Nigerian embassy to get her and her daughter visas to go to his own country. Nothing worked in Tun's favor. He was very disappointed because he was eager to leave Cairo. Felicia told her husband he had to hold on for the right time and to be more patient. She told him she was even tired with the up and down going here and there. So, Tun decided to give up on trying again. She told him when she goes back that she will seek a lawyer and put in the papers for him. One day, Felicia woke up not feeling too good. She had a bad headache and a bad feeling like she wanted to fall. She and Bebe were home alone while her husband went to the market. When he came home, she told him how she felt. He got her some painkillers to take for the headache. Felicia knows that she might be pregnant, but she wants to be sure before saying anything to Tun. She spent one and a half weeks before she went back to Canada. One early morning around 3:00 am, Felicia's phone rang, and it was from back home. They dressed and went to a nearby internet shop to call back home. She gets Iyesha, and she tells her it's Alex. He is in the hospital because he took a pencil and stabbed himself in the neck. Because he said that the teacher had lied to him and that he is tired of getting blamed for everything. Felicia calls the doctor and talks to him. He told her that Alex will be just fine and that she will need to seek help when she gets back because he is going through a lot. Felicia started to cry and told her husband she wanted to change her flight before the time. But later in the evening, her friend, Jo, called her and told her not to worry about Alex, Jay, and Iyesha because they will be okay and that she must enjoy the rest of her time. Felicia was not feeling happy at all. She decided to wait for a couple of days. Felicia is now back home in Canada with her family. They told her everything that happened when she was gone. Even Iyesha takes in and goes to the hospital. She can't believe all these things happened while she was in Cairo. She went to the school to find out what was going on with Alex. She even gets a call from a social worker to come and see her because they got a call about Alex from his school principal. Felicia had so much going on for her at the moment. She took a pregnancy test and found out she is pregnant. Felicia meets with the social worker a week later to discuss Alex's situation. She gives Felicia a number to call, a place to make an appointment for her and Alex to get him help.

# Episode Thirteen

Felicia has so much going on for her this time around. She is pregnant and has to deal with her children, especially Alex. With everything that is going on, Tun wants Felicia to take it easy. Felicia went and did an ultrasound and found out she was having a baby girl. She was happy it was a girl. She calls her husband, Tun, to tell him the good news that they were having a baby girl. He was also happy, but he noticed his wife was not happy. Felicia did something wrong, and she knew it was not right. She has to tell her husband about it. She wondered how he would respond to it. She told him that she had something to tell him, and if he doesn't want to talk to her again, it is okay. Felicia's husband was mad at her for what she did. But later, she apologized to him and said that she was sorry and she will not do it again. That she loved him, and she was going through a lot. Tun told her it's okay, and he forgave her. He decided to buy a ticket for the children and Felicia to revisit him. She prepared for the trip; this time, she is taking Alex and Bebe with her. Alex was excited to go with his mom, this time to Cairo City. Felicia takes them to the doctor to get a shot before leaving the country. Jay was living with her friend, Hope, at the time, and Iyesha was at home. Jo was taking care of her until Felicia came back. Tun was excited to see them and finally meet

Alex. He welcomes Felicia back. She was about five months pregnant. Tun was happy that he was becoming a father of his own. They took the kids around and went to the mall. Felicia just wanted to relax and enjoy the moment with her family. One day, they went to the registrar's office to take out their marriage certificate. They went to the Canadian embassy to see if Tun would be lucky this time around to get a visa to come back to Canada with his wife and the children but were unsuccessful again. The kids and Felicia were enjoying their stay, taking family pictures also. But it was time for them to go back home. It was a sad moment when Felicia and the kids had to say bye to her husband and his friends. They went to the airport, where Felicia didn't want to go. She started to cry and hug him and told him that she loves him and will miss him. Felicia left feeling very sad. They went to catch the plane. The journey is a long way back, from Cairo airport to Amsterdam airport and Toronto, Canada. It takes a day and some hours to reach home. Felicia thanks God that they got back home safely. After Felicia came back home to Canada, before she gave birth to her baby, she went to see a lawyer to help put in her husband's papers. She did everything and sent off the forms to the immigration office. Felicia's husband did all his paperwork and medical forms and sent them in also. Felicia hopes that after the baby is born, he will come. She was supposed to have the baby in the next two months. She had high blood pressure, and the baby was born a week early. It was a girl; healthy and doing great. Felicia called her husband and family to let them know she had the baby and that they were doing great. Two days after being in the hospital, they went back home. Felicia keeps on chatting with her husband on the computer. He was happy to be a father and excited to see his daughter every day. Felicia had her hands full with the help of her friends and Iyesha, who was still living with her and going to school. Felicia continues to take Alex to his program and is still able to manage her home. Felicia is a very wonderful person in and out who loves others and will put her family first in everything she does. Later on, when the baby was about five months, Felicia's husband, Tun, asked her to travel again to Cairo to bring the baby for him to see her. She asked him how she would get the money to buy the tickets for Bebe, the new baby Miracle, and Alex because she is not leaving him behind. Tun told her not to worry because he will get the tickets for them. Felicia wonders where he gets the money to buy the tickets if he doesn't have a job. But she never asked him about it anyway. But she hopes it is their last trip going back there. Felicia went and got a passport for Miracle, but Tun will have to sign the form also. The immigration sent him the form to sign and sent it back to them. They finally went and revisited Tun. He was excited to see his baby daughter Miracle for the first time, face to face. His friends were also excited for him and wished him all the best for his family. He called his family and told them about the baby, and his mom talked to Felicia also. They were happy for both of them. Felicia and the children enjoyed their time with Tun, and they took family photos. He felt sorry that he couldn't come back to Canada with his family. But he said he loves them and will miss them when they leave him.

# Episode Fourteen

After Felicia and the children come back home to Canada from their trip to Cairo, she gets the children settled back to school and daycare. And was staying at home taking care of Miracle; it's been a month and a half since she came back from visiting her husband. She started getting headaches, bad feelings, and no taste. Felicia said to herself, "I hope this is not pregnancy," because she has two young babies; a three-year-old and seven months old. She went to the store and got a pregnancy test kit. She did the test, and it was positive. Felicia started to cry and said, no, how could this happen when she was using protection with her husband. So many things were going through her mind. Did Tun do this to spite me? He is not here; how is she going to take care of three babies on her own? Felicia didn't tell her husband because she was mad at the situation. He will call, and she will refuse to talk to him. He begged her friends to help him talk to her about what is going on with her and what he did. Her friend, Jo, told her to talk to him because he looks like he is going crazy. After two days, when he called, she told him she was pregnant again. And Miracle is only seven months old, and she is still a baby. Tun told her not to worry. He will be with them before the baby is born. Felicia wasn't happy being pregnant so early again. But her friends were there for her and will come by to help her with the children. But for Felicia's husband, everything seems like it is taking too long for him. He calls Felicia time after time to find out what is going on and she must call the immigration in Canada to find out the status of the papers. Felicia will tell him to be patient and wait. He wanted to be in Canada for the birth of his second baby. Finally, after over a year and a month, he received answers from the immigration department in the country where he was staying as a permanent resident of Canada. Tun came in the 5th month in that same year. Felicia's friend drops her at the airport to pick up her husband. They reached the airport, but he was not there yet, so Felicia and the children were there waiting for him to come out. A few minutes later, he came out into the waiting area. Felicia waved at him, and he came over and hugged her and the children. She welcomed him to Canada. Felicia then introduced her friend to her husband. They all left and went home. They were all excited to be together again. Mr. Tun was tired from his trip. He got something to eat and relaxed a bit before taking a bath. Felicia was about six months pregnant when her husband came to Canada to join her and the children. Iyesha was living at home with them, and Max was now working and had moved out on his own. They were a happy family. Then, in the summer, Felicia's youngest brother, Nick, and his girlfriend came to visit them for a month. They met Felicia's husband and liked him. Two weeks later, Felicia was having headaches, and she called her doctor and he told her to go to the hospital. She was 36 weeks pregnant. Felicia, her husband, and Iyesha went to the hospital at the maternal ward and checked in. The nurse gives her a room and a crowd to change into, then the nurse checks her blood pressure, and it is very high, and runs an IV into her hand. The nurse gave her some pain medication to help with the headaches. Felicia's blood pressure was getting worse. The doctor came to see her and examined her; she told Felicia she would break her water and induce labor because her blood pressure is too high. Later that day, Felicia's good friend came to the hospital to be with her for the delivery of the baby. Felicia was having strong contractions, her husband was there holding her hand and talking to her, but the pain was too much for her. Around 8:00 pm, she delivered a healthy baby girl. The baby weighed 6lbs and 3oz and was tall. After two days in the hospital, Felicia and the baby were doing great; discharged from the hospital and went home. Felicia thanked God for a safe delivery and for bringing her back home to her family. Two weeks later, Nick and his girlfriend went back home to their country. Felicia's husband got a job where Max is working. Everything was going well until Felicia noticed a difference with her husband. He will work from Monday to Friday and on weekends; he will be out and will not have time with his family. When Felicia tries talking to him about it, he will ask her if he is her child, and the both of them will always argue with each other. All Felicia wanted from her husband was to spend time with the children. She doesn't mind him going out with his friends. But she wants him sometimes to spend time with his family. One day, her husband forgot his phone at home, and Felicia searched and read his texts. There was a message from one lady calling him the baby and seeing his wife and children. Felicia calls the number and asks the lady why she is calling her husband's baby and what is going on. She tells Felicia that her husband doesn't want her because she is too old for him and met her with four children, and only the last one is his own. She also knows where she lives and what she does for a living. Felicia was shocked that the lady knew a lot about her. She even tells Felicia that she was carrying her husband's child. When Mr. Tun came home, Felicia asked him about the woman and what she told her. It looks like the lady already called him and told him that his wife called her. Because he told Felicia, she got what she asked for through his phone. The two started to argue with each other. Felicia even told him that he is a woman because he can sit down and talk with another woman about her. Everything was just falling apart in the marriage. The lady knew the church where Felicia and the kids were going. Felicia saw a picture of her before and saw her at church; she is married with two children. Felicia tried everything, but her husband was not willing to try with her. When she tries to get him to sit down to talk, he will say that he doesn't have anything to say. There was no communication in the marriage from her husband. Felicia will always feel left out and wonder if he loves her. A couple of months later, Felicia's son, Alex, was getting into trouble at school with other children, and the school called the Children's Aid Society. Then the school called Felicia also, and she went to see the principal about the situation. She gets a call from a social worker. She makes time to talk with Felicia and Alex at home. Felicia usually reads a book and prays with her children every night before bedtime. And hug and kiss each other goodnight. This one night before bed, Bebe went and kissed Alex before bed as usual. She kissed him on the lips, and Felicia's husband, Mr. Tun, saw and accused Alex of kissing Bebe in the mouth. But Alex and Bebe said it was on the lips. Felicia said she didn't see a big deal as he put his tongue into her mouth. Then Mr. Tun and her started arguing about it because he doesn't like Alex. The next day, Mr. Tun called the social worker and went to see her. He told her about what he wanted to talk about Alex in his own words. The social worker even went around the neighborhood looking for information about Alex. Some of the people who did not like him told what they wanted to. A few days later, she went to the doctor to take Alex away when the social workers came to the house. He was home with his two cousins who were visiting and his younger siblings. He told her he is not going anywhere with her because his mom is not home. Later, his mom came home to meet her with two officers in the hallway by her door waiting for her. Felicia saw her and asked her what was going on and why she was here with the police at my door. She said she came to take Alex away from the house to take him to the social service. Alex started to cry, and Felicia asked what he did now, and she told Felicia her husband came to see her. And said he was a bad influence around the rest of the children in the house. The police officer put handcuffs on Alex, who is just ten years old, and took him away like a criminal. Felicia broke down in tears and called her husband to tell him thanks for killing her by making the social worker and the police take her son away in handcuffs like he killed someone. She was so mad at him she lashed out at him and even said things she didn't want to say. He did not come home after two days. Felicia didn't even want to talk to him. She will always be crying and not being happy at all. She went and got a lawyer to help fight in court to get her son back. Alex gets a child lawyer to represent him in court. One day, Felicia got a phone call from the group home that Alex tried to run away twice. She told him not to do it again because it would make the matter worse for him. "I know you want to come home but be a bit patient; everything will work out soon for us," Felicia said. Felicia and the kids and Alex's friends visited him for his 12th birthday at a group home. They were all happy to see him, but he wanted to go home, so Felicia talked to Alex. "I don't like you being here, but you have to hang in there a little while, and your lawyer will get you out of here. Just remember me and your siblings love you and will always do," she said. The judge gives Felicia and the children assets to visit Alex on the weekends at the Children's Aid Society office with supervision. After four months of court with no proof of Alex, he threatens the community and his sisters. He was brought back home to his family. They were all happy to have him back home. Only one thing when he got back; he disliked his stepfather for what he went through. Felicia and her family went for counseling.

# Episode Fifteen

~

One morning, Mr. Tun left home to go to work. He came back home that evening not feeling too good. He went on the couch and rested and said to Felicia that he had a headache. She went and got him two Tylenol, and he took them. After he felt a bit better, he went to take a bath and put on his clothes. Then he started vomiting and said he was not feeling well. He sat in front of the bathroom in the hallway on the floor. Felicia asked if he wanted a cup of tea, then she went and made it and got some rice and meat also to give to him. He just ate a bit and some of the tea. He began to cry, saying that he wanted his mother, but Felicia pampered and assured him that she was there. Then he came down with a fever because he was so hot and said he was feeling cold and was shivering. She rubbed his chest down with Vicks. He went and lay down on the bed. Felicia couldn't sleep. He was still shivering and cold at dawn, so she asked him if he wanted her to call the ambulance, and he replied in the affirmative. She did just that. Felicia called her friend Hope downstairs and asked her to watch the children for her. And she went to the hospital with him in the ambulance. The next morning, Felicia had a doctor's appointment, and she left her husband still in the emergency room to go to her appointment. On her way, she called her husband's mom and told her what was happening. She went back to the hospital. After she finishes her appointment. When she arrived, they got him ready to take upstairs to the ward to stay after settling in. Then, Felicia told him that she was going home to see how the children were doing. Later that evening, she and two of the children went back to the hospital to visit Mr. Tun. He said that the doctor said he has asthma, and they need to run some more tests. Two days later, the three daughters got the flu. She gives them medications to drink for it. She went back to the hospital to visit her husband, and when she went back home, two of her daughters got worse. She just calls a taxi and takes them to the children's hospital. Felicia spent all night there with the girls. They saw a doctor around 4:00 am and got a prescription for the medicine. Felicia went back home that morning around six. She was so tired and went to bed. Her phone rang around 8:30 am. Her husband said that she must come and get him from the hospital because he just got discharged. Felicia gets up, gets ready, and takes a taxi to the hospital to pick up her husband. They went to the drugstore in the hospital and got him some medications. They took a taxi and went back home. Felicia makes something for them to eat. After eating, Mr. Tun got dressed, and Felicia asked him where he was going because he just got out of the hospital. He said he was going to his workplace, and he left. Later that evening, when he got home, Felicia and Tun talked and told him to remember that he had an appointment in two days with the immigration office and how he would get there. He told her to inform Max so that he can take him there. Felicia said she would ask him. The following day, she did ask Max to come early to take Tun to the immigration office. Max assured his mother of his coming. The morning came as planned, Max came to get Tun and Felicia wished him good luck on his test, and he left. A few months later, Felicia noticed her husband started to change at home with her and the children. Every Saturday and Sunday, he will dress and go then come back in the night. She asks him if she did anything wrong; he should let her know or say anything he doesn't like. Tun told Felicia that she is a big woman, and if she does anything wrong, she is old enough to know that. Felicia said to him, "How will I know what I am doing wrong if you don't tell me or if we don't sit down and talk about the situation and the problems between us?" He will say to her that he doesn't have anything to talk about. Felicia told him how she tells him when something is wrong or when he does something wrong. She wants him to be honest with her and tell her. It takes two people to make a relationship work, not one person, and communication. Felicia started to feel like she is losing her husband and her marriage because he is not the same person as before. Sometimes, Felicia will tell her husband about how he doesn't spend time with her and the children. He will tell her that she is not a child. Both of them will always be fighting and saying cruel things to each other. Sometimes, it will happen so fast in front of the children. Felicia knew her marriage was falling apart and was wondering where she went wrong. A couple of days later, Max came to the house to visit Felicia and noticed that she was not looking happy and asked her what was happening. She told him nothing is wrong, but he knows something is not right with his mom. Max told Felicia to talk to him, but she told him she was fine and not too worried. Max asked whether it was her husband. She retorted on why he asked. He told her that day they both went to the immigration office, before coming back home. They went to his workplace; he stayed outside. While her husband went inside and later Tun came out with a lady and his hands around her. The lady saw Max and asked who he was, and he responded that they were friends. Then he kissed her, and they left. Felicia asked Max what he said to him, but he said he didn't ask him anything afterward. Felicia didn't say anything more. Max told his mother that he was leaving for work and encouraged her, then left. Felicia starts to wonder what she is doing wrong in this marriage. She always asked her husband what she was doing wrong, and he could never tell her anything. She does everything as a wife should; take care of the children and the home. She does her duties as a wife. She even tries to communicate with him. One time, Felicia asked her husband how come he never carried her to any of his countries' events or introduced her to any of his friends. He told her that if he was out there and did anything wrong, nobody would come and do his family anything. Or you are ashamed of me. He got angry, and Felicia did not ask anymore. Felicia decided to go back to church and let go of the situation and move on. She gave her life back to Christ and will go to church with the children. After her husband got his citizenship, everything seemed to be getting worse between them and the family. Even the children will tell Felicia they don't like how their daddy is shouting at them. She told them to talk to him about it, and they said that they were afraid. Felicia asked them, "Why? He is your father." She did not tell her husband what the girls said. One month after a Saturday morning, Felicia and her husband were on the bed. She opens a conversation between them, asking him if she is a bad person, and he replies no. Or is she doing something wrong that he doesn't like, and every time she wants them to talk, he doesn't want to? He asked what she wanted him to say, and she also responded that anything at all. And it takes two people in a relationship to communicate, not just one because it will not make any sense at all. She told him there is no food in the house. Then Tun got up, went to shower, and dressed to go out. Felicia didn't say anything. Her friend Hope called her and asked what she was doing. Felicia told her that she wants to go to the grocery, but she doesn't know yet because Tun is getting ready to go out, so she might not get to go today. Tun heard Felicia on the phone talking to someone when he heard his name and asked her who she was talking to about him. He grabbed the phone from her and told her not to talk about him on the phone to her friends. She said that it was Hope asked of him, then he hurriedly banged the door and left. The argument started between Felicia and Tun; he told her she was a foolish woman and started calling each other names. He had a bottle of water in his hand and threw it at Felicia. Felicia was just lashing out with all the stuff she was holding all this while. She even told him that his friends were more important to him than his family and why he hadn't taken his clothes to go and meet them. She even told him what the children said, and he came back inside and asked the girls if he ever shouted at them and they said yes. He said to them, "I don't blame you guys. You all are just like your mother." Felicia went and followed him down in the basement parking lot, and he pushed her, and she fell and hit her head on the ground. She held onto his shirt and did not let him go. They went to her friend Hope in the building. He asks Hope to tell Felicia to let him go. Felicia started to cry and let him go. Hope told them to behave themselves. "Why are you fighting?" Hope asked. Felicia told her what happened. Hope talked to them like she would to her children, but Tun said nothing to talk about, and he left. Felicia then went home, but she was feeling pain in her neck from the fall. She got dressed and left the children and key with Hope and went to the hospital not far from home. At the hospital, she checks in; they check her heart and send her for a head scan, but everything comes back good. They put a brace for her neck and a prescription to get some pain medicine and discharged her. Hope told Felicia that Tun called her and asked if she left the house key with her and where the children were, and she told him that they were with her. He said OKAY and that he will come and collect the key. But he never showed up. Tun did not come back home that night. Felicia called him, but his phone was off. Two weeks later, he came back home and packed a suitcase of clothes. Felicia asked him what this meant. He said he needed some time to think. She asked him where he was going to stay, and he said with a friend. Felicia apologized to him and told him how sorry she was for everything that happened. He said to her, "You get now what you wanted." Then he walked out and left her and the children there. Weeks after weeks, Tun never came back into the house. One day, he came and proposed that they end the marriage. Hurt as Felicia was, she agreed because she did not want to hurt anymore. She has been through too many brutalities from men, and it was time for her to focus on herself and the kids. It was time for her to be happy with her kids since that was where her true joy came from and not from these men who continually use her and hurt her at the end of the day, leaving her battered and broken. Felicia decided to fully give her life to Christ, be with God this time around to know him, worship him in spirit and truth, and do God's things. She needs to give her children a positive and good role model to emulate and fight with her. Felicia enjoys the company of her mother now since she hears from her often and gets more encouragement from her and the other family members. Felicia and the children now go to church. They are learning a lot and are always happy to be in the house of God. She now focuses on her work, loving herself, and being happy. Although the separation has not been fully resolved, she has moved on with her children, and they are living happier than before. No fights, no insults, but rather living in peace.

**<-END->**